THE ART OF
WOOD
FIRED
COOKING

THE ART OF
WOOD
FIRED
COOKING

ANDREA MUGNAINI

WITH JOHN THESS

PHOTOGRAPHS BY JOYCE OUDKERK POOL

GIBBS SMITH
TO ENRICH AND INSPIRE HUMANKIND

First Hardcover and Paperback Editions (published simultaneously)
14 13 12 11 10   5 4 3 2 1

Published by
Gibbs Smith
P.O. Box 667
Layton, Utah 84041

1.800.835.4993 orders
www.gibbs-smith.com

Designed by Debra McQuiston
Printed and bound in China
Gibbs Smith books are printed on either recycled, 100% post-consumer
waste, FSC-certified papers or on paper produced from a 100% certified
sustainable forest/controlled wood source.

Hardback ISBNs
ISBN-13: 978-1-4236-1624-5
ISBN-10: 1-4236-1624-3

Library of Congress Cataloging-in-Publication Data
Mugnaini, Andrea.
  The art of wood-fired cooking / Andrea Mugnaini with John Thess;
photographs by Joyce Oudkerk Pool. — 1st ed.
     p. cm.
  Includes index.
  ISBN-13: 978-1-4236-0653-6 (pbk)
  ISBN-10: 1-4236-0653-1 (pbk)
  1. Barbecue cookery. 2. Cookery, Italian. I. Thess, John. II. Title.
  TX840.B3M82 2010
  641.5'784—dc22
                         2009026445

*To my father, who as a passionate home gardener taught me
that the best results from any kitchen start with the freshest
seasonal ingredients. And to my mother, whose creative cooking throughout my childhood inspired me to trust my senses
and cook with confidence.*

—Andrea Mugnaini
Founder, Mugnaini Imports

contents

How I Became a Pizzaiolo <small>by John Thess, General Manager, Mugnaini Imports</small>

In the early 1980s, I relocated to Santa Cruz, California, to start a bike shop with some friends. The cycling scene was vibrant and alive with ample road riding and mountain biking right outside the door. Although my fantasies of being a racer had long vanished, my friends and I still logged some long, hard miles rewarded by good food and drink. Some months we spent more on food and wine than we did on rent, but the miles kept us lean! It was in this bike shop that

I had the good fortune of selling a road bike to Andrea Mugnaini—an Italian bike, of course. As luck would have it, Andrea became a regular of the shop, and after she left a tip—a bottle of Chianti—I knew I had made a friend.

Soon I became part of the cycling circle Andrea and her husband, Ed, belonged to. Training rides would end with dinner at their house and Andrea effortlessly serving a delicious meal paired with varietals I had never heard of. I was happy to trade my cycling acumen for the culinary education I was sure to receive after each ride. It was during one of these dinners I first heard the plans to install a wood-burning pizza oven in their backyard. And yes, I said those words that everyone reading this book has probably heard: Why would you want to start a fire just to cook a pizza? Little did I know that I would spend ten years answering that question for a living.

I was hired as Andrea's first business manager after her dream became a larger multifaceted company. Naturally, oven sales are the main focus of Mugnaini Imports, but sales back then required a lot of education. Americans' main exposure to cooking with wood stemmed

from barbecues and fireplaces. Many clients had traveling and dining experiences that introduced them to wood-burning ovens, but had no historical or visual reference for what was really going on in that big masonry box. We took sales calls from eager clients who knew they wanted an oven but had no idea of where to put the wood or the food. Andrea was the first to understand that we would need to teach our clients how to use these ovens in order to fulfill her company's mission. Since there was nowhere to send our clients for instruction, that need became the motivation for Mugnaini's Wood-Fired Cooking School.

Andrea had mastered her own oven and offered pizza oven demonstrations that made converts of everyone who attended her classes. With conversational ease, she would fire the oven, hand-stretch pizzas, and pull dishes out of the oven you didn't even see her make. Clients would be delighted and then sometimes frustrated when they could not duplicate her results. Andrea is one of those gifted chefs who cook with intuition and artistry. "In a wood-burning oven you get to cook with your senses," she instructs. Well, I discovered that I am more of a technician than an artist.

The challenge for our classes was to translate Andrea's artistry into tangible steps that could be repeated with similar results. When cooking or entertaining with a wood-burning oven, it is natural to split the duties; one person making pizzas and another baking pizzas. It was clear where I was headed—right to the oven! I had a lot to learn about working a pizza oven in order to meet Andrea's standards. As we say in class,

the most important ingredient to successful cooking in a wood-burning oven is proper firing. It is easy enough to walk up to a readied oven and bake a pizza. You can roast a tender, moist turkey in only a few hours if your oven is just right. However, the question begged: How do you know what "just right" is and how do you make it happen?

What we needed was a foolproof system. Restaurants were a natural resource for oven protocol, but we found out they have a different situation than we do at home. A restaurant's oven is most likely very large and always hot. Mugnaini commercial ovens that have been used during dinner service and then shut down typically retain a temperature of 500ºF or more the next morning, making start-up easy the next day. This is very similar to what Andrea experienced in Italy, since once the oven is fired, it is used daily. The first use may be challenging but then the retained heat makes each consecutive use easier and more consistent. However, for home

use we want to be able to go outside to a cold oven and get it ready in a couple of hours or less, guaranteed. It was time to start testing, documenting and proving the Mugnaini methodology for cooking in a wood-burning pizza oven.

The Mugnaini showroom was converted to a very capable cooking school that still maintained the elegance of a fine dining experience. With four different ovens at my disposal and a steady flow of oven demonstrations, classes, and events, I had the data source I needed for some empirical testing. Cooking environments were documented and then proven again and again. The local invention of the Raytek infrared thermometer enabled me to scientifically track the results we were getting. Not only could I prove what worked for cooking but I was able to analyze the thermal dynamics of the oven itself. We changed the way we fired our ovens and developed a system that ensured deep, even heat in three simple steps. We also isolated distinct cooking environments that are easily identified visually. The guesswork was

gone and the Mugnaini method was established. Now, in the course of a three-hour class, clients could learn the basics of wood-fired cooking and go home enabled with the tools necessary to confidently use their ovens.

Whether we are catering an event in wine country for hundreds of people, cooking at home, or teaching a class, we use these same techniques every time. We have trained thousands of homeowners, chefs, and even our competition in the Mugnaini method. It is flattering to read our words in books and on websites of others, and we feel this is a testament to what we teach. I encourage you to go through this book as if you are attending one of our classes. Follow the steps and you'll get great results. Our style is fast and efficient. Our cooking temperatures are high and we use a lot of live flame. This is not the norm for every chef, but these techniques have been well vetted. I know you will be thrilled as you transform simple foods into surprisingly delicious meals with the basic recipes found in this book. Get the tools, learn the rules, and the art will follow.

Introduction by Andrea Mugnaini, Founder, Mugnaini Imports

Living in culinary Italy as an Italian wine importer gave me the opportunity to experience the live and interactive style of cooking with a wood-burning oven. In 1989, I decided to dedicate Mugnaini Imports to work exclusively with wood-burning ovens, which allowed me to bring this heartfelt style of cooking to American homes as well as share it with my own friends and family. My research on ovens led me to choose Refrattari Valoriani, the inventors of Italy's original modular pizza oven. This is the wood-burning oven that long ago signaled the change in the average Italian family's reliance upon communal ovens to home ovens constructed in their own backyards.

Family, friends, and even the manufacturer thought I was crazy to try and sell pizza ovens to Americans. Why would anyone want to go back to starting a fire in order to cook a meal? That was old-fashioned and inconvenient! However, the benefits I experienced kept me focused and I knew I was not alone. I believed there were a lot of people like me who like to cook and entertain at home, who enjoy the sensuous process of food preparation and presenting delicious meals.

When I opened my first school in Watsonville, California, the goal was to accommodate the enormous need for instruction that had become evident. There was no written record of how to use an oven. The lessons I received in Italy—"Just put the fire here, hold your hand inside and count to ten, and then put the food there"—certainly were not

People who like to cook and entertain at home enjoy the sensuous process of food preparation and presenting delicious meals.

going to suffice. My staff and I were inundated with emergency calls from apprehensive clients who were in the middle of a pizza party, or those attempting to roast a holiday turkey the next day without specific instructions.

My first solution was to install four working wood-fired ovens and bring in guest chefs, culinary instructors, and cookbook authors to teach classes. While that kept us busy and the students entertained, they left without the specific skills and techniques necessary to duplicate those beautiful recipes in their wood-fired oven. It became clear to me that Mugnaini needed to teach our clients how to first fire their ovens and then manage them to master any given recipe.

Soon a curriculum was developed that offered instruction in how to fire a wood-burning oven for a variety of cooking styles based on our personal experiences and research. I became an interpreter of old-world cooking, translating techniques into recipes that worked with our ovens using ingredients that are widely available. The best part is that it worked for homeowners of all skill levels. Proud students routinely email photos or call us, giddy with excitement over the outcome of a meal.

A pleasant surprise for me was how teaching professionally has become the single most enjoyable and rewarding part of my work. I communicate with people worldwide and love teaching them how to maximize the benefits from their oven. Through this book I can extend these relationships and provide instruction to many others seeking to more fully enjoy their wood-burning oven. As you progress through the pages of this book, I hope you are rewarded by the art of wood-fired cooking as much as I am.

Mugnaini Wood-Fired Cooking School

The Art of Wood-Fired Cooking is the culmination of Andrea Mugnaini's twenty-year career educating Americans about wood-fired ovens. This book represents the teaching arm of Mugnaini that was first started in the Watsonville, California, headquarters and has expanded to include Cucina Mugnaini in Healdsburg, California, and Fattoria Usignoli in Tuscany. Up until the writing of this book, Mugnaini cooking classes were primarily reserved for our clients in order to offer them specific oven instruction.

It is assumed that if you are reading this book you already own a wood-burning oven (or soon will) and are looking to enhance your experience with it. We have debunked many myths and misconceptions over the years in order to create an effective and successful method of cooking. The following points reflect the findings, philosophy, and results from our test kitchen. As you proceed through this book, we are confident that you, too, will discover the distinct advantages to cooking in a wood-burning pizza oven.

The most important step to any recipe is properly firing your oven. You do not need "wood-fired oven" recipes in order to cook. The recipes in this book form a foundation for a variety of cooking styles in a wood-fired pizza oven. Once these skills are mastered you can reach into your library of cookbooks to apply any given recipe.

A wood-fired oven is a moist cooking environment, not a dry heat as some state. Seasoned hardwood contains up to 20 percent water content. A small three-pound log has the potential to release 1 cup of water into the oven when burned.

A wood-fired oven allows you to cook differently than you may be accustomed to. The high heat and live flame speeds the pace of cooking. The retained heat allows you to cook overnight with no flame. The open door offers accessibility to monitor your food and engages all of your senses while you cook.

The success of your cooking and the quality of your outcome starts before the actual cooking process. Getting to know your food vendors and educating yourself about ingredients is equally as important as following the steps of a recipe. Discuss the seasonally available fish with your fishmonger. Talk to the farmers at your local farmers market. Ask for samples of cheeses and fruits and make informed decisions before you buy.

Have fun and cook often. Trust your instincts and use the full cycle of heat your oven offers. Wood-fired ovens like to work and offer heat throughout the night and even into the next morning.

The Wood-Burning Oven Today

Steeped in centuries of tradition, the wood-burning pizza oven is a majestic testimony to the beauty and goodness of open-hearth cooking. There is no disguising the purity and authenticity of nature's finest ingredients cooked next to a roaring fire. Taken from the field to the hearth, foods are able to maintain their individual characteristics. Dynamic results are obtained using the simplest seasonings and techniques without the need to mask flavors with a complicated sauce.

With no moving parts or electronics to control it, the wood-fired oven at first appears to be a relic of the past. Yet, it is still the most sophisticated and versatile appliance in your kitchen. Your oven can harness the power of fire and reach temperatures no gas oven can match. Control the flame and you can create multiple cooking environments. Once you master the fire, your oven will faithfully replicate your favorite meals.

More Than Just a Pizza Oven

Today the pizza oven takes on a larger role than that of any other cooking appliance. These masonry monuments to food often anchor an outdoor kitchen. The open hearth becomes a focal point in many beautifully designed indoor kitchens. The live, interactive style of cooking creates a fun atmosphere, and the oven actually becomes an entertainment center for your guests. Beyond all of these benefits, though, is what an oven can do for food.

When firing an oven in the Mugnaini method, you will be engaging in flame-affected cooking. The rolling flame from the fire brings searing heat while the 1,200-degree coal bed provides the power to fully penetrate even large cuts of meat. All of the old clichés about "sealing in the juices" and "locking in the flavors" truly happen at these temperatures. High-heat roasting of meats and vegetables brings caramelization not found in conventional ovens. Looking to cook rotisserie style? The oven is a static rotisserie with high heat radiating from all sides, reducing the need to rotate food. The floor of the oven acts like an infinitely adjustable cooktop; simply place a pan on it and cook. Need more heat? Move towards the fire. Too hot? Move away from the fire. It is that simple. There is no need to dig a pit to cook a whole pig overnight when you can roast a thirty pounder in three hours. Want to barbecue? Pull the coals forward and insert a Tuscan grill. And what other appliance can bake a Neapolitan pizza in ninety seconds?

Wood-Burning Pizza Oven Defined

With the recent interest in pizza ovens, there is a variety of appliances that claim to be such. This cookbook is based on the Italian wood-burning pizza oven that we define as a refractory clay bake chamber (dome) with a firebrick floor. The internal shape is similar to an igloo that is insulated and surrounded by masonry or steel. The oven has one door and an exhaust vent (chimney) located near the opening. A fire is made inside the oven and food is cooked directly next to the fire with the door primarily left open.

There are many oven brands that follow this formula. Your oven may be square or tunnel shaped, lightweight, or an enormous masonry structure. As long as the inside is made of masonry (not steel) and you have a chimney, the following instructions will work for you. The oven's shape, materials, and installation method all play a part in how it will function; but remember, you have only one oven to master—yours!

Pizza Oven Dynamics

A wood-burning oven uses five types of heat for cooking. First, the heat is transferred to the oven via fire. The flames of the fire heat the dome. When the wood burns down to coals, these red-hot coals transfer heat into the floor. Once the oven is heated, the same forces are used for cooking.

1. Heating by conduction is offered by the firebrick floor. When you place something cold on top of something hot, the transfer of heat is referred to as conduction. Pizza and breads are placed directly on the floor to bake. The oven floor can also be used like a stovetop. Simply place a pan on the floor to sauté or pan sear.

2. Radiant heat is provided by the dome. The fierce energy of the fire is absorbed by the clay dome and stored for hours of cooking. It then softly radiates throughout the entire cooking chamber, whether the fire is going or not. This is the primary heat source for baking or roasting.

3. Burning logs creates a large flame rolling across the top of the dome, for a broiler effect inside the oven. This intense flame attacks the surface of food and is utilized to brown and caramelize meats and vegetables. It is essential for fast-baked pizza.

4. The convection flow of heat is created by the shape of the dome and the live fire placed on the side of the oven. You can actually see the smoke spin inside our ovens. This convection flow makes for even browning and is accentuated in round ovens. If your oven is tunnel shaped or square, make sure to pay more attention to turning dishes while roasting to ensure even cooking.

5. The high heat of the coal bed is the true power source in the oven. Food is always moved in relation to the coal bed. You can also move the coals forward to create a pure grilling environment.

An understanding of these heat sources will be beneficial as you fire your oven and create different cooking environments.

How to Fire a Wood-Burning Oven

The task of heating an oven is a simple matter of burning wood down to coals and moving the fire around the oven using a three-step process. With a little attention to detail, this technique will bring an oven up to temperature quickly and evenly. You will then be able to regulate the oven into five distinct cooking environments by monitoring the size of the flame and the floor temperature.

The Essentials for Fire

We keep three items on hand for starting the fire and working the oven.

• *Weber brand fire starters.* These paraffin-based nontoxic cubes ignite immediately to the strike of a match and offer 10 minutes of flame. They are essential for starting fires and come in handy any time the oven has lost its flame. They are available in many hardware stores or from www.mugnaini.com.

• *Hardwood kindling.* We use kiln-dried hardwood kindling that is boxed in 12-inch lengths and is approximately 1 inch square. This kindling is ideal for starting or refreshing a fire. It may be difficult to source in your area, but you might try your fire wood vendor or a cabinet maker, as their scrap is used to make kindling.

• *Double-split seasoned hardwood.* Our bottom line is simple. We want wood that will burn easily, offer a large flame, and establish a stable coal bed. We use oak and almond wood in our school. We suggest you source local hardwood and buy a smaller quantity to first verify the quality. We have used many types of wood over the years and have never changed any of the firing methods or cooking methods because of the type of wood.

Double-split refers to wood that has typically been split once and then split again, ideally into a 4-inch triangle. Let your wood purveyor know you are using the wood for cooking, not for a fireplace. Lengths of 12–16 inches work well, with the shorter length ideal for smaller ovens measuring 32 inches in diameter or less. You will find that the smaller size "cooking" logs offer more control over the size of the flame. Sourcing good wood is the best investment you can make toward your success with a wood-fired oven!

CAUTION: Indoor oven owners should place great emphasis on using hardwood only. The smoke in the longer chimneys cools with the moisture in the air to form creosote, which can cause a flue fire. Follow your oven manufacturer's operating instructions and have your chimney cleaned regularly by a certified chimney sweep.

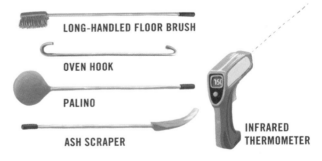

LONG-HANDLED FLOOR BRUSH
OVEN HOOK
PALINO
ASH SCRAPER
INFRARED THERMOMETER

Oven Tools

There are only two tools that are essential, and they are usually supplied with an oven.

• *Long-handled metal peel (palino):* Used to turn pizzas in the oven but serves double duty for moving wood.

• *Long-handled floor brush:* Used to sweep the ash into the fire and keep the floor clean.

The following oven tools have been developed to make working an oven easier and safer. We recommend and use every one but they are not essential.

• *Ash scraper:* Long-handled tool with a curved blade designed to move coals.

- *Oven hook:* Long steel tube with a hook on each end to reach deep into an oven to retrieve pans.
- *Log grate:* Steel stand that lives in the fire and keeps wood propped on an angle to enhance burning.
- *Oven mitts:* Insulated mitts that extend up to the elbow and have a vapor barrier to stop steam burns.
- *Infrared thermometer:* Handheld thermometer that reads the surface temperature of the oven floor.

Working with Fire

We have found that some students have never lit a fire, while others have grown up with wood stoves. For those unfamiliar with the subtleties of burning wood or using a wood-burning oven, we offer a little primer and some cautions. The old hands may pick up some tips or jump ahead to our firing procedures.

CAUTION: Follow your oven manufacturer's curing instructions before firing your oven per these instructions. Thermal shock can occur, creating a crack in the clay dome even after curing. While this is not catastrophic, it is not desirable and can be avoided by gradually heating your oven and not over firing. If flames are extending past the oven opening and up the exhaust flue, you are over firing the oven.

NOTE: If the wood is popping, sizzling, smoking heavily, and not lighting easily, you probably have green wood. Add kindling to keep the fire going so the green wood will dry out and burn.

The elements of a fire: Firestarters are used to ignite the kindling. Kindling's job is solely to ignite the hardwood. The hardwood offers the live flame and burns down to coals. The coals eventually burn down to ash.

The fire needs to breathe: The combustion air for the fire flows through the mouth of the oven. The oven door needs to remain open for the fire to burn. Closing the door to hold the heat in has the opposite effect and chokes the fire down. If wood is not burning, reposition the log slightly and elevate one end on another piece of wood for better airflow. A little kindling goes a long way;

practice with smaller amounts until you are familiar with the wood's potential and add kindling sparingly.

Moving wood inside the oven: We position the wood using the metal peel. Alternatively, oven mitts allow you to reach into a hot oven, but never throw wood inside the oven as you may damage the walls.

Identifying a hot oven: Every time an oven is fired, the smoke from the fire will coat the dome with a layer of black soot that burns off around 900ºF. The burning off of this soot indicates the oven is coming up to temperature. No matter how long the fire has burned or how much wood has been used, you need to burn the black soot off the entire dome before you are ready to cook.

Firing Procedures

Three steps to firing an oven: The goal for firing an oven is to saturate the dome with heat, saturate the floor with heat, and establish a mature fire identified by a bed of red hot coals and a live flame. The length of time to bring an oven up to temperature is determined by how long it takes your wood to burn down to coals and the thickness of your oven walls. Visual cues will let you know when each step is completed.

Step 1. The Center Burn (about 20 minutes)

First we want to introduce an appropriate amount of heat into the oven and establish some coals. The door can be placed outside the arch at a slight angle to

CENTER BURN

control smoke rollout inherent with a cold oven. Make sure the fire is getting enough air to burn strongly; remove the door if necessary.

• Start in the front center of the oven within arms reach. Place three firestarter cubes lengthwise on the oven floor spaced between two good-sized pieces of kindling. The kindling needs to be large enough to elevate the wood pile, allowing for oxygen to reach the fire. Use small logs if necessary. Light the firestarters with a match.

• Place a handful of kindling across (perpendicular to) the first two pieces of kindling.

• Place two small hardwood logs across (perpendicular to) the kindling pile and top with one or two more small hardwood logs, depending on the size of your oven. Maintain this crossing pattern so that the air can circulate through the wood.

• Push the woodpile deeper into the oven with a long-handled peel. You can either push on the bottom kindling pieces or come under them and lift slightly to move the entire woodpile as one. It is okay if the woodpile falls apart. We want the fire just back of the center of the oven. Flames should reach the top of the dome and cascade to the sides. Give the wood a chance to do its work. However, if the kindling has burned up and the logs are not burning, add more kindling and firestarters to get the flame back to the top of the dome.

• Keep the fire burning and expect to add several more pieces of wood to maintain a large flame reaching the top of the dome. We want to burn wood in this manner until there is a buildup of red hot coals and you see a minimum 8-inch circle on the dome, directly above the fire, that is no longer black.

Step 2. The Perimeter Burn (about 30–45 minutes)

At this point we decide which side of the oven we want to bank the fire on and which side of the oven we want to cook the food on. The goal of the perimeter burn is to preheat the cooking side of the oven. If you are right handed, you will probably feel most

PERIMETER BURN

comfortable with a fire on your left side and the food inside the oven on your right.

• Using your long-handled metal peel or ash scraper, push the fire (burning logs and red hot coals) from the center of the oven to the perimeter, close to the oven walls on the cooking side of the oven (see illustration). The fire should wrap around two-thirds of the circumference of the oven. Start close to the oven opening and line the oven walls past the center mark. Leave the center open.

• Add enough wood and kindling to have three logs burning. As logs burn up they break down into coals. Expect to add another three logs. Leave some room between the wood and the oven walls, being careful not to smother the fire.

• Maintain a flame that reaches across the top of the dome. We call this a preheat flame and this is the most important step in heating an oven. Start slowly until you know your oven's limits and the power of your wood.

BANKING THE FIRE

Burn in this manner until you have burned the black soot off this side of the oven.

CAUTION: Do not have more than three to four logs burning at the same time until you have proven your oven is large enough and capable to handle that much fire. If flames reach out beyond the mouth of the oven and up into the chimney, you are over firing the oven which may send hot embers out the top of a short chimney! Knock the fire down and back off your quantity of wood.

Step 3. Banking the Fire (about 10–15 minutes)

Now we are ready to move the fire to the cooking position. We follow the Italian method of banking the fire on the side of the oven, not in the back. The fire should be only an arm's length inside the oven. Using a log grate will allow the wood to be elevated above the coal bed for better aeration.

• Using your long-handled metal peel or ash scraper, push just the logs to the opposite side of the oven and prop them up on the log grate. Next spread the red hot coals evenly across the middle of the floor, pulling them away from the oven walls. These coals will drive heat deep into the floor. Add wood to maintain a preheat flame and burn off the remaining black on the dome.

• Using your long-handled metal peel or ash scraper, move all the coals from the center of the oven to the fire. Push the coals under the logs and against the oven wall. The coal bed should be oblong like a football, extending over one-fourth of the floor (8–12 inches) from the wall and tapered back on each side.

• Use the floor brush to sweep any ash into the fire. Pay careful attention to cleaning along the wall and just inside the oven opening. If necessary, wrap a damp cloth around the brush to help clean the floor.

Congratulations! You Are Ready to Cook!

The preheated oven should have a dome void of black, a bed of coals, and one to two logs burning. The door may be left outside the arch at an angle to put the oven into a "holding" mode. Remember, the fire still needs oxygen, so do not close the door completely, and keep the fire going by adding a piece of wood every 20 minutes until you are ready to cook.

Mastering Your Oven

As you learn the steps to firing an oven, you will discover the best timing for your particular oven. Thanks to retained heat, an oven used the day before typically heats up in half the time. However, if you find your oven dome turns black quickly upon starting to cook, then you need to extend your perimeter burn time. If your floor cools down quickly, then leave the coals on the floor longer after banking the fire. Conversely, some floors can get overheated; you should skip spreading the coals if this is the case with your oven. With experience, this process will become efficient and predictable.

Regulating an Oven for Cooking

The beauty of a well designed oven is its versatility. The ability to use one appliance for a full complement of cooking styles such as roasting, braising, grilling, baking, and, of course, making authentic Neapolitan pizza is unique to the wood-burning pizza oven. We refer to five distinct oven environments in order to maximize these different cooking methods.

The key is achieving a balance of heat inside the oven and proper firing is crucial to attaining this. No matter what cooking method you are planning to use, you must first bring the oven up to pizza temperature and then let it drop down to the appropriate environment. Once an oven is fully saturated with heat, each of these environments can be identified by the floor temperature and the size of the flame.

Reading the Oven Temperature

The only tool we use for measuring temperature is the infrared thermometer. The only place we check is the floor. For accuracy, hold the thermometer at the oven opening. Standing too far back will only give an average of the entire floor. Pull the trigger, look for the red laser dot, and slowly pan across the oven floor. We use the thermometer as a tool for learning how to identify cooking environments and the temperature as a gauge for a range of cooking, not as a hard number. Variances of 25 degrees are inconsequential if you have the proper preheat and fire.

Heat Zones Inside the Oven

Every oven will have heat zones, and we use these to our advantage. It is hottest next to the fire and gradually reduces in heat as you move toward the opposite oven wall. It will be hotter deep in the back of the oven and cooler as you move toward the oven opening. You can use your thermometer to identify the heat zones in your oven, which may vary as much as 100°F from the "hot" side to the "cold" side. Rarely do we cook in the

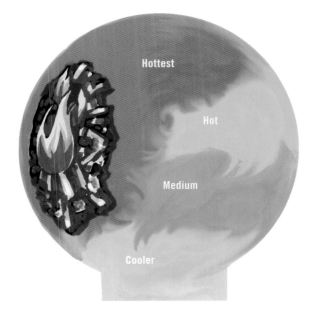

HEAT ZONES

mouth of the oven, but the coolest zone, opposite the fire tucked just inside the mouth of the oven, is a valuable spot and is ideal for roasting fish while the vegetable course is cooking closer to the fire. Once we start cooking, we stop looking at the temperature and instead pay attention to the food. Unlike a conventional oven, a wood-burning oven allows you to watch the food cook and observe what is happening to quickly learn whether you need to move towards the heat or away from it.

Oven Environments for Cooking

You will notice a ratio between the floor temperature and the size of the flame in the various environments we describe. As the floor gets hotter the flame gets larger. This ensures the balance to cook food evenly, top and bottom.

Pizza Oven Environment. Floor temperature of 650–750°F with a flame rolling to the middle of the dome.

The pizza oven environment is running an oven at

PIZZA OVEN

ROASTING OVEN

maximum temperature and is used for a variety of foods besides pizza. The entire dome should be void of any black soot, the coal bed should extend 8–10 inches from the oven wall, and a live flame should be rolling to the midpoint in the dome. The middle of the oven floor should read between 650–750°F. The door remains off.

Pizzas are cooked deep in the oven and alongside the coal bed. A thin Neapolitan style pizza will bake in 1½–2 minutes at 750°F. The same pizza will bake in 2½–3 minutes at 650°F. Baking time is a matter of preference and can be adjusted for personal tastes. Other foods cook at 650°F with a corresponding flame that rolls to the middle of the oven.

When firing an oven in the pizza oven range, expect to add one to two pieces of wood every 20 minutes to maintain the live flame.

Roasting Oven Environment. Floor temperature of 550°F with a vertical flame extending up the wall only.

The roasting oven environment relies more on the

radiant heat retained in the dome than live flame, so a thorough preheat is important. Start with the pizza oven environment and let the oven drop down in temperature by not stoking the fire. It is crucial that a live flame be maintained, so this is when smaller logs are used. Depending on your oven, the door may be placed in the oven opening at an angle to damp down the oven. If your oven fills with smoke, then remove the door or open it a bit more to increase the air flow. (The hot smoke in the oven will impart a creosote flavor.)

The roasting environment is very versatile, allowing for adjustments depending upon the menu item. When roasting meats or poultry, we start at 600°F and then let the temperature drop slightly, maintaining 550°F. Initial browning or searing of meats is done by adding wood and creating a rolling flame. For poultry we save the browning for last and use an aluminum foil tent, leaving the tent open on both ends to allow for air flow. For braising, a pan can be sealed after browning with

BAKE OVEN

GRILLING OVEN

a lid or aluminum foil. Thicker or rolled pizza will bake in approximately 5 minutes at this temperature. Sauté pans or other cookware can be placed directly on the oven floor.

When cooking in a roasting oven environment, you still need to maintain the fire. Check the floor temperature first before adding wood. When in doubt or if the coal bed is starting to shrink, add wood, leaving the door fully open until the wood has ignited.

Bake Oven Environment. Floor temperature of 350–450°F with hot coals but no live flame.

The bake oven environment relies solely on the radiant heat retained in the oven. Simply let the fire go out and the floor temperature will drop correspondingly. If the temperature is dropping too fast, fully close the door to maintain the heat. When baking, the door is either slightly open or fully closed, depending on bake times.

The bake oven environment is typically used for desserts, but it is appropriate for pasta dishes or even to slowly roast a turkey breast. Long bake times and delicate foods benefit from the use of terra-cotta cookware that offers a layer of insulation and softens the heat. Our terra-cotta bean pots do an extraordinary job with cannellini beans cooking overnight. The fire might be out, but there is still potential for cooking.

When using the bake oven environment you still have conductive heat from the floor and radiant heat

from the dome. If the floor is too hot, place your dish on an inverted sheet pan to temporarily offer some insulation. If your food is browning too quickly, cover with an aluminum foil tent. If the coal bed is still live, don't close the door all the way or you may impart a smoky flavor. Use the heat zones in the oven to adjust the cooking temperature.

Ideally there is no live fire while in the bake oven environment. If it is time to bake and there is a live fire, bury any burning logs in the coal bed to extinguish them.

Grilling Oven Environment. Live coals only.

The grilling oven environment is the only time the oven doesn't need to be preheated. From a cold oven, establish a center burn until you have abundant red hot coals. From a preheated oven, use your metal peel or ash scraper to dig into the coal bed and pull forward only the red hot coals. Mound the coals in the archway of the oven right underneath the exhaust flue, making sure not to spill any coals outside of the oven. Any burning logs can be pushed to the back of the oven.

NOTE: Our Tuscan Grill is a two-piece system with a stand that straddles the coals and a grill with a handle that sits on top of the stand. The grill is used much like any barbecue and is available at www.mugnaini.com.

Allow the grill to get hot before adding food. Any flare-ups can be knocked down with the hook or metal peel. Vary the height of the coals according to the desired temperature.

Grilling in a pizza oven has several advantages that make it the better barbecue. Foremost, you are grilling over 1200ºF red hot coals; this is when you really taste the wood. You are conveniently positioned at eye level and can pull the grill forward, off the heat, to turn or to season. All of the smoke travels right up the oven flue and the food you grill is not exposed to cold air on one side.

When grilling in the sequence of a meal, it is appropriate to fire the oven for one course and then pull the coals forward to set up for grilling. After grilling, push the coals back, reposition the wood, and sweep the floor. It should only take 10 minutes to start a fire and regulate the oven again.

Bread Oven Environment. Floor temperature of 450–550ºF, empty oven.

The bread oven environment is unique as it relies on radiant heat from the dome and conductive heat from the floor with an absence of any fire or coals. The oven is fired in the same manner with the goal of having all of the wood burn down to embers at the same time. The heating time depends on the amount of bread you wish to bake, either one full oven or several batches of bread. The longer you need the heat, the longer you need to fire your oven. This environment can also be established at the end of a meal.

From a preheated oven, dome void of any black, spread the coals evenly across the floor, favoring the front of the oven. If you have already been cooking, then remove the coals from where the fire was. With no live flame, close the door. The oven will regulate to an even temperature throughout. Only experience will educate you on how long your oven needs to regulate and how long it will hold the temperature.

If you need the oven to cool down faster, open the door for 10 minutes at a time. With the door open, the convection flow starts even without a flame and cools

BREAD OVEN

the floor. This will create an imbalance, so be sure to close the door again to regulate the oven. Check the floor temperature only after the door has been closed a minimum of 10 minutes, as the heat will migrate down.

To prepare for bread baking, remove the door and pull out all of the coals using a metal peel or ash scraper. Be sure to have a metal container with a lid for this job, as the coals may still be hot and could flare up in the presence of oxygen. Use protective gloves to store the container safely on a noncombustible surface. Use the floor brush to sweep the ashes out of the oven. Use a damp cotton mop or a damp towel wrapped around the brush to clean the floor. Plan on the oven losing 50 degrees during this operation. Place the door on the oven and let it regulate for at least 10 minutes and then take a floor temperature reading.

Bread can be placed on the oven floor in the same manner as pizza or can be baked in bread pans. A cast-iron pan may be filled with water and placed on the oven floor to introduce moisture to the oven. We use a garden sprayer to mist the oven after the last loaves have been peeled. The oven will not be adversely affected if you need to open the door to check on progress or rotate loaves.

To judge whether bread is done, we use the following criteria.

Length of bake: In general terms, a ciabatta bakes in

30–35 minutes at 525ºF, a one-pound loaf should take 45 minutes at 475ºF, and a focaccia 30–40 minutes at 400ºF.

Color: It is natural to bake until you achieve the color you want, but you may be fooled. Color is determined by temperature, so if you bake at a hotter temperature you will get more color, but the loaf may not be fully cooked through.

Internal temperature: An instant-read thermometer can be used to measure internal temperature of the bread. Look for 190–200ºF for a fully baked loaf.

When converting bread recipes for use in a wood-burning oven, the only adjustment you need to make is the bake temperature. Add 75–100ºF to your recipe when using the infrared thermometer to read the floor temperature. Then be sure to take notes based on your results and adjust accordingly.

A bread baker can also take advantage of the cycle of heat in an oven. Start your first bake with a wet bread like a baguette or ciabatta that bakes quickly at a high temperature. Then the larger loaves can be baked using the bulk of the oven's energy, followed by sweet breads that can't tolerate more than 450ºF. By varying the types of bread you bake, you get the most from your efforts.

Oven Management

Once you have heated your oven and regulated the proper cooking environment, you will still need to add wood. Since there is no industry standard on the size of wood or how long it will burn, you will find you need to make a judgment call at times. This guide will help you finesse your oven like a pro.

Never add wood with food in the oven. Try to time your wood management and floor sweeping to coincide with an empty oven, either between pizzas or while checking the temperature of your food.

If you feel the oven needs more heat, first agitate the coal bed and reposition the wood. Quite often that is all you need to do to increase heat or achieve a larger flame.

Observe the size of the coal bed to determine whether to add one or two pieces of wood. If the coal bed is starting to shrink, add more wood.

If the oven is getting too hot and you still need some live flame, try using kindling rather than a log. Using large logs in small ovens can overwhelm the oven with coals. Kindling will offer the live flame you need without appreciably increasing the size of the coal bed.

If the oven has lost too much heat or if the oven is not hot enough for the dish you are attempting to cook, stop cooking, remove your food, and establish a preheat flame. By adding some kindling and one to two logs, you will stoke up a large flame that rolls across the dome from one side to the other. You will not be able to cook, but you will raise the oven temperature 100ºF in 10 minutes. This little break will mean all the difference between success and a meal that suffered from being in the oven too long at too low a temperature.

If you are planning on roasting a big turkey or hosting a large party, it is advantageous to fire the oven the day before your event. All it takes is burning four to five logs in the center burn to drive some heat deep into the oven and make the next day's firing that much easier.

If you have not used your oven for some time or the oven has been exposed to a heavy rainy season, excessive moisture may have built up in the masonry structure and insulation around your clay components. A "wet" oven performs poorly until all of the moisture has been cooked out. A wet oven will not hold the heat you are accustomed to and the dome may turn black even with a proper preheat. A long, slow firing over several days will cure this problem.

Recipe Conversions

The temperatures called out in recipes based on cooking in a conventional gas oven are reading the ambient air in the oven. We add 75–100 degrees to those temperatures in order to reference the floor temperature of a wood-fired oven. So if a recipe calls for roasting at 425°F, then we want the floor temperature to read 525°F. In addition, the bake time can be expected to be one-third faster.

Suitable Cookware

Remember, a wood-burning pizza oven is still an oven, so the cookware we choose is what is appropriate for the menu item we are cooking. There is a strategy for cookware and a few rules we follow.
• Glass or Teflon coated cookware is not appropriate for a wood-burning oven, nor is any cookware with a wooden or plastic handle.
• Stainless steel conducts heat well and is great for pan browning. Rugged commercial grade roasting pans with handles, sauté pans, and pots with tight-fitting lids all work well.
• Stainless steel paella pans are a house favorite at Mugnaini for many recipes.
• Terra-cotta or any other ceramic cookware offers an insulating quality and is the choice for delicate foods or menu items that will be in the oven for longer times at lower temperatures.
• Cast-iron conducts too much heat and can get red hot and unusable at high temperatures. Use it carefully or not at all. Blue steel is a better alternative.

Closing Down Your Oven

When it is time to stop cooking, simply close the oven door. As a rule, we do not close the door if there is a live flame, but closing the door will retain the most heat for your next cooking session.

Maintenance

Wood-burning ovens self clean with each subsequent firing. However, you will need to dispose of the ashes leftover from cooking. A dedicated metal can with a tight-fitting lid is recommended. Indoor ovens should have the chimney inspected and potentially cleaned yearly or after every cord of wood is burned. Outdoor ovens can be monitored by observing build up on the spark arrestor (chimney cap screen). Follow your oven manufacturer's maintenance instructions.

PIZZA, CALZONES, AND FLATBREAD

There is no disguising the purity and authenticity of nature's finest ingredients cooked next to a roaring fire.

How to Make Pizza

Clients often come to school perceiving that pizza dough is difficult to make, time consuming, and complicated. We demystify this immediately with our simple, easy-to-follow formulas that consistently achieve great results. Four ingredients and a drizzle of olive oil is all that is required to produce pizza dough that is delicious, well structured, and performs well in the high heat of a wood-burning oven.

Also, it is good to keep in mind that wood-fired pizzas only take a couple of minutes to bake, so when you are ready to start, be sure to have everything you are going to put on your pizza prepared and in position. This means you will need to

give advance thought to the types of pizza you want to prepare and whether or not your pizzas will be served as appetizers or the main course.

As a rule of thumb, wood-fired pizzas are best kept lightly topped. Combine ingredients to ensure that every pizza has its own unique identity and flavor. Resist the urge to use every ingredient you prepared on the same pizza. This allows you to progressively present your guests with a greater variety of flavors throughout your service.

If you are serving pizza as an appetizer, we suggest offering a smaller pizza topped with smaller sized ingredients, making it easy for guests to enjoy as finger food. A 5-ounce dough ball stretched to 8 inches and then cut into 8 slices is ideal. At our catering events, we serve this size pizza directly from the wooden peel with cocktail napkins. Guests are delighted and can't wait to see what flavor the next pizza will be!

When hosting a progressive pizza party, we start with the lighter appetizer pizzas and build up to the bigger, bolder flavors. For entrée-style pizza we recommend a slightly larger 7-ounce dough ball stretched to 10 inches and left uncut. Serve this pizza on a flat pizza plate with a knife and fork, just like they serve it in Italy.

Essential Equipment

We recommend investing in a commercial dough box for holding/proofing the dough balls, a dough scraper/bench knife, and several high-quality wooden peels with beveled edges. These items will make your pizza service efficient and ensure good results. The dough boxes hold fifteen dough balls each and can be stacked and transported safely, and they keep the dough from developing a dry skin. The wooden peels become our work surface to make pizza and are then used to transfer the pizza to the oven floor. We even use them for passing pizza at a party, so it's good to have at least four of them on hand.

Fresh Homemade Dough

Making dough at home can be easy and effective. We use the same formula, only altering the amount of yeast, to create doughs with different fermentation times. Just select one of the following recipes that best suits your entertainment schedule. If it is 3 p.m. and you want pizza for dinner, then make the 3-Hour Dough (page 38). If it is Friday and you are having a large crowd over on the weekend, use the 24-hour or 48-hour dough variations to give yourself time to prepare. These dough recipes will provide sophisticated yet forgiving dough that is delicious and consistent. However, one of the fundamentals of dough is that structure and the complexity of flavors is increased with longer fermentation times. So when you have the time, try experimenting with each one.

Rolling Dough Balls

Once the dough has proofed, it is time to roll out dough balls. If the dough has been refrigerated, allow extra time for the dough to come to room temperature, about 1½ hours. Remove the dough from the bowl and turn it out onto the work surface. Roll the dough into a log and, using a dough scraper, divide into equal portions according to the batch size. Roll the individual portions into balls using the palms of your hands to press into the dough while making a circular motion. Do not use flour unless the dough is very sticky, as the tension between the work surface and your hand will form the ball. As the ball forms, use less tension and position your fingers like a cage to lightly roll the dough ball until you achieve a smooth, even texture on the outside. Place in a dough box and cover. Repeat with the rest of the dough and place dough box in a warm location to rest.

NOTE FROM THE AUTHOR: Every cookbook and instructional video on pizza shows perfectly round, smooth dough balls turned into perfectly round discs ready for pizza. In reality it takes much practice to achieve this, but it is not magic. Be patient with the lumpy dough balls and irregular shapes. As you begin to work with dough, you will learn to identify the stages of development and feel the tension as you stretch the

doughs. This learning curve is worth the effort, since using a rolling pin presses the air out, producing a crust that is dense and that restricts the hot air from moving easily through the dough. Also, the use of a rolling pin flattens the perimeter edge of the pizza and it burns quickly. Hand-stretched dough results in a crust that is lighter and more aerated. The air moving through the pizza makes it cook faster, creating a texture that is light and tender. Have fun and remember, the irregular-shaped pizzas taste just as good!

Resting the Dough

After rolling the dough balls and transferring them to the proofing box, they will need some time to rest. This rest period allows the gluten complex to relax, which will make opening the dough easier. After they rest, they should feel soft, supple, and, when poked with a finger, the indent does not spring back. This will take about 20–30 minutes depending on the temperature—less time for hot weather and more for cold weather.

If the dough is stiff, will not stretch easily, and springs back, then it needs to relax longer. Don't fight it; just give the dough more time to rest and possibly move the dough box to a warmer place for a few minutes. If the dough balls have been left to relax too long, they will start to over proof and lose their structure. These balls will have lost their shape, flattened out, and developed large gas bubbles. The easiest way to prevent this is to set the dough balls in the refrigerator when they start to develop gas bubbles. The dough can still be used or re-rolled, but the crust will be some-what compromised in its texture. With time, you will be able to recognize these phases of the dough and be able to intuitively adjust the placement of the dough boxes to either speed up or slow down the pace of the dough. Also, when making pizza over a long period of time, you will find you can roll the dough balls at intervals according to the pace of the party.

Opening the Dough

With a hot oven, relaxed dough, and your ingredients ready, it is time to stretch your first pizza.

Ready your work surface. Place a wooden peel on a flat surface and dust it with about 2 tablespoons flour concentrated in the middle of the peel.

Transfer the dough ball. Use your dough scraper to scoop a dough ball from the dough box. Try to maintain

the round shape and place it on the floured portion of the peel. Turn the dough over so both sides are floured.

Flatten the dough ball into a round disc. Apply direct overhead pressure using flat hands and pressing gently but firmly, allowing the dough to maintain its round shape. This step has the most impact on the final shape of your pizza. Resist the urge to stretch laterally as this will overstretch the center of the dough.

The first pull. Pick up the dough with both hands, holding your fingers under the dough and your thumbs

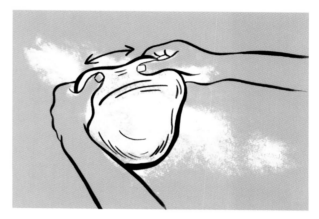

on top just inside the outside edge. Your hands should be next to each other at the 12:00 position. Grip the dough and pull your hands apart several inches to the 10:00 and 2:00 positions. You want to pull with conviction but not a yanking motion. Simply pull once and then place the dough flat on the peel but still in your hands. With time you will be able to judge the tension in your dough. If the dough is too stiff, it may start to tear. If you go too far you may create a thin spot.

The second pull. Now shift your left hand next to your right hand; move the right hand back a few inches and

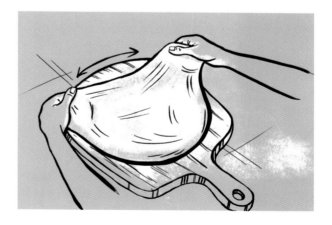

pull again. As you move around the perimeter of the dough, the pulls get longer and your right hand moves farther back. Short little pulls will result in a rumpled edge with a thick center. Do not hold the dough vertically or it will stretch out of shape. Lift only slightly above the peel and drop the dough back onto the peel, lightly dusting it with flour at the same time. When working quickly, we actually hear the dough slap against the peel.

Working the perimeter. At this point, we now work our hands around the outside edge of the pizza like a wheel, keeping our fingers on the bottom and our thumbs on top to form the edge. As you pull the dough, there is a feeling that the edge is getting squeezed between the thumb and first finger. We want to leave the edge undisturbed and approximately ¼ inch thick. This edge will increase in size when baked and create a protective barrier to keep all moist ingredients inside. The pulls get larger as your fingers sense the thick spots and stretch the dough more. Only a few times around the dough should finish the job—pulling too many times will overwork the dough.

There is a tendency to want to shape the dough, but this is unnecessary if you start with a round disc and just pull outward. Any holes can be patched by folding dough over to build up thickness. Before topping the pizza, make sure there is ample flour underneath to allow it to slide easily. Fresh dough can stick to the peel, so shake the peel to verify the dough is sliding before topping.

Baking Pizza

Once the pizza is topped, it is ready to bake. Have your oven readied per the pizza oven environment, the floor swept clean, and the long-handled metal peel at hand. We use the wooden peel to transfer the pizza to the oven using a shuffleboard action and the metal peel to turn the pizza in relation to the fire to bake.

Transfer the Pizza

Place the wooden peel through the oven opening and allow the beveled front edge to come in contact with the oven floor. With a smooth motion, push the peel inwards and then quickly pull back. Emphasize the backwards motion, hopefully leaving the pizza on the oven floor. With some practice this becomes a natural motion.

If the pizza is sticking to the peel, do not attempt to transfer the pizza. Instead, lift up on the edge of the pizza and dust the peel with some flour. Continue doing this until the pizza moves freely and then transfer to the oven.

First Position

The cooking zone for a pizza is deep in the oven next to the fire. Regardless of where your pizza landed, do not move it until you see the rim form around the outer edge. The soft dough will tear if you try to move the pizza before the bottom sets. This only takes 10 seconds, so be patient. Then, if necessary, gently slide the metal peel under the pizza, lift, and place it in the cooking zone.

Pizza Turning Technique

The metal peel is used to move and turn a pizza. The tendency is to try to steer the pizza with the peel. In actuality it is a two-step process. First, place half the peel under one side of the pizza. Next, lift 2–3 inches and pull straight back and watch the pizza spin. Now let the pizza down and come underneath the middle of the

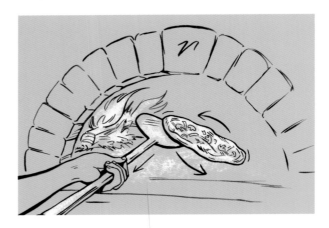

pizza with the whole peel. Lift up, move, and pull back swiftly, leaving the pizza in position.

Second Position

The bulk of the cooking is done in the first position.

After approximately 1 minute, observe the side of the pizza next to the fire. The edge will start to brown and even blister. Reach in with the metal peel and turn the pizza toward you, allowing you to see the browning. The pizza only needs to be turned two to three times for even baking, so you will be baking one-fourth to one-third at a time. For the best bake, avoid turning the pizza too soon or too many times.

Third/Fourth Position

Turn the pizza again when the side next to the fire is nicely browned. This is the time when you make a decision about temperature. Lift slightly under the pizza to observe the browning on the bottom and look at the top. If you feel the pizza is getting overcooked, then move it away from the fire for the remaining cook time. If you need more heat, push the pizza deeper into the oven. When you can lift the pizza from the front edge and the pizza stays stiff and does not fold, then the crust is set.

A Properly Baked Pizza

We want to see a crust that is evenly browned with some black blisters, bubbly cheese, and a bottom that is seared with black charred bits. The pizza should feel light when picked up and not fold in the middle.

We suggest you start baking pizza with a floor temperature of 650°F and a flame just rolling to the center of the oven. The bake time will be 2½–3 minutes and is very manageable and appropriate for even a thicker topped pizza. With practice, you may wish to raise the temperature to 750°F by adding wood and try for a 90-second bake time. Pizza Margherita and some appetizer pizzas benefit from this hotter, faster bake time.

Multiple Pizzas

Naturally, it is best to bake one pizza at a time until you become proficient. When you are ready for multiple pizzas, you will want to get a rotation going. Three pizzas are very effective with two alongside the coal bed and one deep in the oven away from the fire. It is a matter of choice which direction you move, but it is natural to change positions each time you turn a pizza. By leaving an open space in the oven, one pizza can be moved over, making room for the others to turn. It is fair game to move a pizza to the cold spot in the oven temporarily in order to not burn it and concentrate on the others.

Pizza Oven Management

Remember to keep a large flame burning at all times to keep the oven balanced and to return heat to the floor. A hot floor with no flame will burn the crust before the toppings are cooked. If the bottom is burned, you may conclude the oven is too hot. In fact, the oven actually needs more flame so that the top cooks at the same rate as the bottom. Likewise, if the bottom is not cooking, check the floor temperature and follow the oven management techniques in Regulating an Oven for Cooking (page 24).

If you have burned a pizza beyond recognition, if it turned upside down, or tore in the middle, making a mess on the floor, then just throw it into the fire. Any errant toppings or extra flour can be swept into the fire as well. Reach into the coal bed with the metal peel and spread some hot coals on the mess. Give it about 10 minutes to burn off and then scrape the mess into the fire and sweep the floor. Do not cook on top of burned food—it will ruin a nice pizza.

3-Hour Pizza Dough

Yields approximately 32 ounces of dough, about 4 to 5 (10-inch) pizzas. These portions double, triple, and quadruple successfully.

1½ cups warm water, divided
1 teaspoon active dry yeast
4 cups "00" flour
1 teaspoon salt
1 teaspoon olive oil

Place ¼ cup warm water in a small bowl and sprinkle with the yeast. Let sit for 5 minutes or until yeast is hydrated and creamy. This will allow the yeast to be quickly absorbed by the flour.

Hand Method

Place flour and salt in a mixing bowl. Add yeast mixture and remaining water, stirring while pressing the back of the spoon against the sides of the bowl. Mix until dough takes on a "shaggy" look, then drizzle with oil. Stir to incorporate oil, pulling dough into a ball, and then turn out onto a lightly floured work surface.

Knead for 5 minutes, dusting with flour if necessary. If dough feels dry and difficult to knead, cover and let rest for 10 minutes; resume kneading. If dough is sticking to the work surface, use a dough scraper to lift dough and add flour. (The dough should feel moist but not sticky. If the dough is too wet and builds up on your hands, add flour 1 tablespoon at a time.) After the initial 5 minutes of kneading, cover dough and let rest 20 minutes. Knead for 3–5 minutes more and then place dough in a lightly oiled bowl and cover with plastic wrap. Set aside at room temperature for 2½ hours or until doubled in size.

Mixer Method

Place flour, salt, yeast mixture, and remaining water in mixer bowl fitted with a dough hook. Mix on low speed for 2 minutes to combine. If the dough appears too wet and sticky and is not combining, add flour 1 tablespoon at a time while mixing until dough takes on a "shaggy" appearance. Drizzle with oil and mix for 2 minutes more. Dough should form a smooth ball and clear the sides of the bowl. Turn mixer off, cover top of bowl with plastic wrap, and let rest for 20 minutes. Resume mixing on medium-low speed for 3 minutes, or until dough forms a smooth ball, clearing sides of bowl. Place in a lightly oiled bowl and cover with plastic wrap. Let sit at room temperature for 2½ hours or until doubled in size.

24-Hour Pizza Dough

Follow directions for 3-Hour Pizza Dough. Refrigerate up to 24 hours. Remember to allow several hours for pizza dough to warm to room temperature before using.

48-Hour Pizza Dough

Follow directions for 3-Hour Pizza Dough, but adjust yeast measurement to ½ teaspoon. Refrigerate up to 48 hours. Remember to allow several hours for pizza dough to warm to room temperature before using.

Cheese Calzone

1/3 cup fresh ricotta cheese, drained
1/4 cup diced fresh mozzarella cheese
1/4 cup grated Gruyère cheese
1 teaspoon finely chopped fresh parsley
1 teaspoon chiffonade fresh basil
Freshly ground black pepper
Pinch of freshly grated nutmeg
1/4 cup diced prosciutto cotto (optional)
1 (8- to 10-ounce) Pizza Dough ball (page 38)

Combine all ingredients except dough in a bowl and mix well. Mound mixture onto one half of the stretched dough towards the center. Lift the remaining half of the dough over the filling, fitting the edges together. Pinch the edges well to seal. Place calzone in oven opposite the fire and toward the foreground. Bake for about 5 minutes, or until you see it puff and stiffen. Pull forward and pierce with the tip of a sharp knife to release steam. Brush with olive oil and return to oven to continue baking for another 2–3 minutes.

Sausage and Vegetable Calzone

1/4 cup chopped roasted sweet red bell pepper
1/4 cup sautéed spinach, drained well
1/4 pound spicy Italian sausage, sautéed and
    cooled to room temperature
1/3 cup fresh ricotta, drained
1/2 cup diced fresh mozzarella
1/4 cup grated fontina
1 tablespoon grated pecorino
1 teaspoon fresh oregano leaves, whole
1 (8- to 10-ounce) Pizza Dough ball (page 38)

Combine all ingredients except dough in a bowl and mix well. Mound mixture onto one half of the stretched dough towards the center. Lift the remaining half of the dough over the filling, fitting the edges together. Pinch the edges well to seal. Place calzone in oven opposite the fire and toward the foreground. Bake for about 5 minutes, or until you see it puff and stiffen. Pull forward and pierce with the tip of a sharp knife to release steam. Brush with olive oil and return to oven to continue baking for another 2–3 minutes.

NOTE FROM THE AUTHOR: Good "00" pizza flour is now available in many grocery stores and specialty markets. All-purpose flour does not have enough protein to make good pizza dough. Bread flour often has too much protein but is a better choice than all-purpose. The ideal flour for pizza dough has approximately 10.5 percent protein and the flour is finely ground. The "00" designation refers to the fine grind that yields a soft mouthfeel and the 10.5 percent protein content develops a strong dough. Working with dough is a tactile learning experience. If you don't have "pizza flour," use what you have access to and get started. The sooner you get your hands into some dough, the faster you will learn to make great pizza.

Margherita

1 (6- to 8-ounce) Pizza Dough ball (page 38)
¼ cup canned San Marzano or other
   good-quality tomatoes, undrained,
   crushed or coarsely chopped
Fresh basil leaves
2 ounces fresh mozzarella cheese, sliced
Pinch of grated pecorino cheese
Extra virgin olive oil

Place tomatoes in center of dough and with the back of a spoon, spread in a circular motion, keeping 1 inch around outer edge. Tear basil leaves and scatter over tomatoes. Top with mozzarella and pecorino, and drizzle with oil. Slide in oven and bake for 1½–2 minutes.

Schiacciata with Rosemary

1 teaspoon finely chopped fresh rosemary
1 (6- to 8-ounce) Pizza Dough ball (page 38)
Extra virgin olive oil

Sprinkle rosemary onto pizza dough and bake in oven for about 90 seconds. Remove and drizzle with oil.

NOTE FROM THE AUTHOR: When your pizza recipe calls for tomato sauce, we recommend using the Neapolitan standard of canned San Marzano tomatoes, uncooked and either crushed by hand or put through a food mill. The San Marzano is a variety of plum tomato grown near Naples, Italy, and prized for their superior flavor. By starting with a pure tomato base rather than a cooked sauce, you can season the tomatoes differently for individual pizza recipes.

Smoked Mozzarella and Shiitake Mushrooms

1/3 cup grated smoked mozzarella
1 (6- to 8-ounce) Pizza Dough ball (page 38)
1/2 cup very thinly sliced raw shiitake
   mushrooms
1/2 teaspoon chopped tarragon
1/2 teaspoon chopped parsley
1 tablespoon grated Parmigiano-Reggiano cheese

Sprinkle mozzarella over pizza dough and top with mushrooms. Sprinkle with herbs and Parmigiano-Reggiano. Slide in oven and bake for 1 1/2–2 minutes.

Fresh Mozzarella with Salt-Cured Capers and Kalamata Olives

1/4 cup canned San Marzano or other
   good-quality tomatoes, undrained,
   crushed or coarsely chopped
1 (6- to 8-ounce) Pizza Dough ball (page 38)
1 teaspoon dry oregano
2 tablespoons salt-cured capers, soaked and
   drained
2 tablespoons coarsely chopped kalamata olives
2 ounces fresh mozzarella cheese, sliced
Extra virgin olive oil

Place tomatoes in center of dough and with the back of a spoon, spread in a circular motion, keeping about 1 inch around outer edge. Sprinkle with oregano, capers, and olives; top with mozzarella. Drizzle with oil. Slide into oven and bake for 2–3 minutes.

Caramelized Onion, Fresh Thyme, and Blue Cheese

2 tablespoons olive oil
1 medium white onion, halved and thinly sliced
Pinch of salt
1 teaspoon chopped fresh thyme
1 (6- to 8-ounce) Pizza Dough ball (page 38)
2 tablespoons crumbled blue cheese

Heat olive oil in a sauté pan over low heat. Add onion and salt and cook slowly for 45–50 minutes until caramelized. Do not raise heat and "fry" onion. Remove from heat and add thyme. Spread onion-herb mixture over dough and top with blue cheese. Slide in oven and bake for 1½–2 minutes.

Spinach, Ricotta, and Pancetta

¼ cup canned San Marzano or other
    good-quality tomatoes, undrained,
    crushed or coarsely chopped
1 (6- to 8-ounce) Pizza Dough ball (page 38)
⅓ cup fresh ricotta
⅓ cup sautéed spinach*
1 teaspoon freshly grated Parmigiano-Reggiano
    cheese
Pinch of freshly grated nutmeg
3 thin slices pancetta, julienned
Extra virgin olive oil

Place tomatoes in center of dough and with the back of a spoon, spread in a circular motion, keeping 1 inch around outer edge. Dollop ricotta and sprinkle spinach over top. Sprinkle with Parmigiano-Reggiano, nutmeg, and pancetta. Drizzle with oil. Slide in oven and bake for 2–3 minutes.

*Place 2 cups spinach onto sheet pan, drizzle with olive oil, and add 1 small clove garlic, minced, and a pinch of kosher salt. Place in oven and cook until wilted, about 1–2 minutes. Remove and set aside.

Fromage Blanc and Smoked Salmon

⅓ cup fromage blanc
1 (6- to 8-ounce) Pizza Dough ball (page 38)
4 thin slices smoked salmon
½ small lemon
1 tablespoon chopped fresh dill

Using the back of a spoon, spread fromage blanc onto dough. Set pizza in oven and bake thoroughly for about 2 minutes. Remove from oven, lay salmon on pizza, then squeeze fresh lemon juice over top. Sprinkle with dill.

Marinated Eggplant, Goat Cheese, Fresh Oregano, and Lemon

1 (6- to 8-ounce) Pizza Dough ball (page 38)
2 ounces fresh mozzarella, sliced
4 slices marinated eggplant*
1 teaspoon chopped fresh oregano
½ teaspoon lemon zest
2 tablespoons chopped kalamata olives
Pinch of red pepper flakes
2 ounces goat cheese
Extra virgin olive oil

Top dough with mozzarella and arrange eggplant slices over top. Sprinkle with oregano, lemon zest, olives, and red pepper flakes. Top with crumbles of goat cheese. Drizzle with oil. Slide into oven and bake for 2–3 minutes. Makes

*Peel an eggplant and slice lengthwise or in rounds about ¼ inch thick. Place onto an oiled sheet pan and roast in oven with a large flame (best during the perimeter burn of the startup time), turning to brown lightly on both sides. Remove, sprinkle with salt, and drizzle generously with olive oil. Set aside for use on pizza.

Roasted Asparagus, Fontina, and Truffle Oil

⅓ cup grated fontina cheese
1 (6- to 8-ounce) Pizza Dough ball (page 38)
6 roasted asparagus spears, sliced on the diagonal into 2-inch sections
½ teaspoon finely chopped fresh parsley
1 teaspoon freshly grated Parmigiano-Reggiano cheese
Truffle oil

Sprinkle fontina over dough, and then top with the asparagus, parsley, and Parmigiano-Reggiano. Slide into oven and bake for 1½–2 minutes. Remove and drizzle with truffle oil.

Roasted Pepper Sauce, Provolone, Sausage, and Broccoli Rabe

¼ cup Roasted Pepper Sauce (see below)
1 (6- to 8-ounce) Pizza Dough ball (page 38)
⅓ cup grated provolone cheese
¼ cup parcooked spicy Italian pork sausage
¼ cup sautéed broccoli rabe*

Place Roasted Pepper Sauce in center of dough and with the back of a spoon, spread in a circular motion, keeping 1 inch around the outer edge. Top with provolone, sausage, and broccoli rabe. Bake for 2–3 minutes.

Roasted Pepper Sauce

Place 2 red bell peppers on a sheet pan and set into oven with a large flame (best during the perimeter burn of the startup time). Blacken skin on peppers, turning once or twice to evenly char. Do not overcook peppers or they will dehydrate. Peppers should be blackened on the outside with a tender and juicy interior.

Remove from oven, place in a bowl and let rest, uncovered, until cool enough to touch. Once cool, remove peppers from bowl and reserve any accumulated juices. Slip the charred skins from peppers and remove seeds. Do not rinse with water. Place skinned peppers and any juice remaining in the bowl of a food processor. Process until smooth. Season with salt to taste. (May be done 2 days in advance and stored in refrigerator.)

*Coarsely chop a bunch of broccoli rabe, place into boiling salted water, and cook for 3 minutes. Remove, drain, and rinse under cold water. Place 2 tablespoons olive oil in a sauté pan with 1 clove garlic, minced, and 1 anchovy. Heat through for about 1 minute. Add broccoli rabe and cook, stirring to mix well for about 2 minutes. (May be done 2 days in advance and stored in the refrigerator.)

SEAFOOD

Wood-Roasted Butterflied Shrimp

This is another recipe that works well as both an appetizer and a first plate. It uses the freshest wild shrimp, butterflied and cooked with the simplest of seasonings to enhance natural sweetness. It makes a beautiful presentation for a dish that pleases everyone.

ROASTING OVEN ENVIRONMENT

2 pounds large shrimp, shell on (about 30)
1 teaspoon sea salt
1 teaspoon lemon zest
3 tablespoons fresh lemon juice
2 tablespoons olive oil

Remove the shell up to the tail segment and remove the vein from the shrimp. Cut through the shrimp to open like a book, being careful not to cut all the way through. Repeat until all shrimp are butterflied.

Place shrimp in a medium bowl and add the remaining ingredients; toss together. Cover and refrigerate for 1 hour. Remove from the refrigerator and place onto a sheet pan, cut side down, with the tail curled over the shrimp. Place in oven and roast for 3–5 minutes, or until pink and firm to the touch.

SERVES 6–8 AS AN APPETIZER OR 4 AS A FIRST PLATE

Pan-Seared Ahi with Sesame Seed Crust

This quickly seared, deliciously seasoned tuna is great as an appetizer served with your favorite dipping sauce. It also works well as a first plate served on a salad dressed with fresh citrus vinaigrette. Always purchase the freshest sushi-grade tuna for the best results.

PIZZA OVEN ENVIRONMENT

6 (1-inch-thick) ahi steaks, about 6 ounces each
3 teaspoons sesame oil, divided
1 tablespoon black sesame seeds
1 tablespoon white sesame seeds

Place a sauté pan large enough to hold all the ahi steaks in one layer into the oven and heat well for about 5 minutes.

While pan is heating, lightly brush steaks using 2 teaspoons sesame oil. Combine the sesame seeds on a plate. Set steaks on plate with sesame seeds, turning and pressing to coat both sides. When steaks are coated, add remaining oil to hot pan; heat well and add steaks. Cook for 45 seconds, turn over, and cook for 45 seconds more. Remove and slice thinly to serve.

SERVES 12 AS AN APPETIZER OR 6 AS A FIRST PLATE

Roasted Halibut Ligurian Style

Color, flavor, and texture—this dish has it all. Not to mention, this recipe will also serve a large crowd with ease. Potatoes and sauce may be prepared in advance and then everything can be assembled in seconds.

ROASTING OVEN ENVIRONMENT

1½ pounds Yukon gold potatoes, cut into ¼-inch rounds

⅓ cup plus 1 tablespoon olive oil

4 teaspoons salt, divided

½ teaspoon pepper, divided

2 baskets small cherry tomatoes

6 (1½-inch-thick) halibut fillets, about 6 ounces each

½ cup Basil Pesto (see below)

BASIL PESTO

2 cups fresh basil leaves

½ cup extra virgin olive oil

3 tablespoons pine nuts

2 cloves garlic, peeled and coarsely chopped

1 teaspoon fine table salt

2 tablespoons water

Toss the potatoes with ⅓ cup oil, 2 teaspoons salt, and ¼ teaspoon pepper.

In a separate bowl, toss the tomatoes with the remaining oil, ½ teaspoon salt, and remaining pepper.

Oil a sheet pan and shingle potatoes so the entire surface is covered. Place in the oven and cook for about 12 minutes, or until lightly browned and softened; remove and set aside.

Place tomatoes on a sheet pan, set in oven, and cook for 5–6 minutes, or until tomatoes are softened and slightly charred; remove and set aside.

Place fish on top of the roasted potatoes; sprinkle each fillet with ¼ teaspoon salt. Return to oven and cook for 12 minutes, or until the fish flakes easily with a fork.

Remove from oven and top each fillet with roasted cherry tomatoes; drizzle with pesto.

Basil Pesto

Place the basil, oil, pine nuts, garlic, salt, and water in a blender; blend until smooth.

SERVES 6

Fish in Acqua Pazza

This is the easiest fish recipe ever. We have been preparing this dish for years in our cooking classes and students always have great success and are surprised by how flavorful it is for being so very simple. Serve with your favorite rice.

ROASTING OVEN ENVIRONMENT

2 cups chopped tomatoes (about 4 Roma tomatoes)
2 tablespoons extra virgin olive oil
1 teaspoon salt, divided
½ teaspoon freshly ground black pepper, divided
4 red snapper fillets, about 5 to 6 ounces each
½ cup water
1 lemon, thinly sliced
1 tablespoon chopped parsley

Place the tomatoes, oil, ½ teaspoon salt, and ¼ teaspoon pepper in a bowl; toss to combine.

Arrange the fillets in a single layer in a large sauté pan. Add the water and season the fish with remaining salt and pepper. Top with the tomato mixture and lemon slices.

Place the pan in the oven, uncovered, for 4 minutes. Cover the pan with a lid and cook 8 minutes more, or until the fish is just cooked through. With a spatula, remove the fish and toppings to a platter and cover to keep warm.

Return the sauté pan to the oven and cook, uncovered, for 4–5 minutes, or until the sauce reduces and starts to thicken. To serve, spoon sauce over fish and sprinkle with parsley.

SERVES 4

Oven-Roasted Clams

This is a great combination of sweet with a little spice. We serve this in a large paella pan straight from the oven. Be sure to include some grilled rustic bread to enjoy the flavorful juices!

ROASTING OVEN ENVIRONMENT

5 pounds clams

⅓ cup diced pancetta

1 tablespoon olive oil

2 cloves garlic, finely chopped

Pinch of red pepper flakes

1½ cups fish stock

1 cup white wine

½ cup canned San Marzano or other good-quality tomatoes, crushed

1 tablespoon chopped fresh oregano

In a large bowl, combine the clams and enough cold water to cover. Refrigerate for about 20 minutes. Remove and gently lift clams out of the soaking water, leaving the sand and grit in the bottom of the bowl. Rinse clams and set aside.

Place the pancetta and oil in a shallow pan (a stainless steel paella pan works well). Set in the oven and cook until the pancetta begins to brown. Add the garlic and pepper flakes and cook for 30 seconds more. Do not burn the garlic. Add the clams, fish stock, wine, tomatoes, and oregano. Cover the pan tightly with foil and place back in the oven. Cook for 20–30 minutes, stirring halfway through the cooking time. Clams are cooked when they have all opened; discard any unopened clams. Serve in a bowl with the broth.

SERVES 8

Zuppa di Pesce

Another great dish for entertaining. The broth may be prepared a day in advance and kept in the refrigerator. The combination of seafood can vary based on the freshest choices available to you. Use a beautiful large pot for cooking and bring directly to the table. Be sure to ladle the servings into individual bowls so guests don't miss any of the sweet, fresh broth.

ROASTING OVEN ENVIRONMENT

2 pounds mussels, scrubbed and debearded

3 pounds clams

2 pounds white fish (snapper, cod, and haddock)

1 cup white wine

4 cloves garlic, finely chopped

Juice of 2 lemons

3 tablespoons chopped parsley, divided

2 cups roughly chopped canned San Marzano or other good-quality tomatoes, with juice

3–4 cups Fish Broth (see below)

1 pound shrimp, shelled and cleaned (reserve shells for broth)

1 pound calamari, sliced into rings

FISH BROTH

¼ cup extra virgin olive oil

1 bulb fennel, coarsely chopped

1 onion, quartered

2 stalks celery, coarsely chopped

2 whole cloves garlic

1 carrot, coarsely chopped

1 dry red chile

Pinch of saffron threads

Reserved shrimp shells and/or fish heads and frames

3 quarts cold water or more to cover

Place the mussels, clams, white fish, wine, garlic, lemon juice, 2 tablespoons parsley, and tomatoes in a large pot. Stir to combine. Add Fish Broth to just cover.

Cover pot with foil and seal well. Place in oven and cook for about 20 minutes, or until clams and mussels are open. Discard any unopened shellfish. Add shrimp and calamari and cook for 2–3 minutes. Remove, add remaining parsley, and serve.

Fish Broth

Place oil in a stockpot. Add the fennel, onion, celery, garlic, carrot, chile, and saffron and sauté for 5 minutes. Add the shrimp shells and/or fish frames and cover with cold water. Simmer briskly for 20 minutes. Strain through a colander and reserve liquid. Any leftover broth can be frozen in a ziplock plastic bag for later use.

SERVES 12

Black Cod En Papillote

The technique of using parchment paper to wrap ingredients helps to ensure a moist, tender fish that is seasoned with the juices of fresh spring vegetables. The presentation is beautiful and elegant, with each guest receiving his or her own flavorful package.

BAKE OVEN ENVIRONMENT

6 heart-shaped pieces parchment paper
5 tablespoons extra virgin olive oil, divided
1 bulb fennel, fronds removed
1 medium leek
6 stalks asparagus
3 medium carrots, grated
3 teaspoons sea salt, divided
½ cup white wine
6 black cod fillets, about 6 ounces each
½ teaspoon freshly ground black pepper
6 teaspoons butter
12 slices lemon

Brush parchment pieces lightly using 2 tablespoons of the oil.

Cut fennel bulb in half and then julienne. Repeat with the leek and asparagus. (Be sure that the vegetables are cut very thin, as the fish cooks quickly.) Toss all the vegetables with the remaining oil and 2 teaspoons salt. Evenly divide the vegetables in the center of each piece of parchment. Pour 2 teaspoons wine over each pile of vegetables. Place a piece of fish on top and season with remaining salt and pepper. Top each piece of fish with 1 teaspoon butter and 2 lemon slices.

Fold each piece of parchment over and fold the edges to seal; press tightly. Place packages on two sheet pans and cook in oven for 12–15 minutes. The parchment will puff and brown. (To check doneness, take one package out and carefully open a small portion. Insert a small knife to check the fish. It will flake easily when done.) Remove from oven and serve immediately, slicing an opening in the top of each package to release the aromatic steam.

SERVES 6

Oysters Stuffed with Sautéed Spinach and Melted Jack Cheese

This recipe is an elegant choice for an appetizer that can be cooked quickly once guests have arrived and are starting to gather around the oven. Have everything ready and prepped for assembly. We feature this appetizer served with a sparkling wine in our holiday entertaining classes.

PIZZA OVEN ENVIRONMENT

Rock salt
1 dozen fresh small oysters (such as Kumomoto)
½ pound fresh spinach
2 tablespoons extra virgin olive oil
¼ teaspoon salt
4 ounces Monterey Jack cheese
Freshly grated nutmeg

Pour a layer of rock salt in a sheet pan to cover bottom. Shuck oysters and set on rock salt. Place in refrigerator while preparing remaining ingredients.

Place spinach on a sheet pan, drizzle with oil, and sprinkle with salt. Place in oven and cook until just wilted, about 1–2 minutes. Remove and set aside to cool.

Thinly slice cheese into pieces small enough to fit on opened oysters. Top each oyster with a small amount of spinach followed by a slice of cheese. Sprinkle lightly with nutmeg. Cook in oven just until cheese is melted, about 2 minutes, and remove. Be careful not to cook the oyster. The cheese and spinach should be warm with a cold briny oyster beneath.

SERVES 6 AS AN APPETIZER OR 4 AS A FIRST PLATE

Grilled Swordfish in Agrodolce

Thinly sliced swordfish grilled quickly over very hot coals is delicious by itself. However, combined with this sweet and tangy sauce, it becomes a more special and flavorful dish. The sauce may be prepared a day in advance, making this even easier for entertaining.

GRILLING ENVIRONMENT FOR FISH
ROASTING ENVIRONMENT FOR SAUCE

¼ cup golden raisins
½ cup hot water
2 tablespoons olive oil
1 small white onion, quartered and thinly sliced
2 large cloves garlic, sliced
2 tablespoons pine nuts
2 tablespoons capers, rinsed
¼ teaspoon dry oregano
⅛ teaspoon red pepper flakes
1 bay leaf
1 cup white wine
1 (14-ounce) can San Marzano or other good-
    quality tomatoes, drained and crushed
3 tablespoons white wine vinegar
1 tablespoon sugar
½ teaspoon salt
1 teaspoon chopped parsley
4 (½-inch-thick) swordfish steaks, about
    6 ounces each
Salt and pepper

Place raisins in a small bowl, cover with hot water, and set aside.

Heat a sauté pan with oil in the oven. Add onion and cook until softened and lightly browned. Add garlic, pine nuts, capers, oregano, red pepper flakes, and bay leaf; cook, stirring for about 2 minutes. Add wine and cook for 2–3 minutes, or until wine is almost evaporated. Add the tomatoes, raisins with soaking liquid, vinegar, sugar, and salt. Cook for 15 minutes. Sauce should be thickened slightly. Remove from oven, stir in parsley, and set aside; keep warm.

Pull hot coals forward in oven. Oil a Mugnaini Tuscan Grill and set over coals to heat.

Season swordfish with salt and pepper and grill for 3 minutes. Turn and grill for 2 minutes more on second side. Remove and serve topped with the sauce.

SERVES 4

Wood-Roasted Side of Salmon

We have all experienced cooking fish where one end is overcooked and the opposite end is undercooked. In our cooking classes, students follow these instructions for rotating the pan to achieve an evenly cooked, delicious side of fish.

ROASTING OVEN ENVIRONMENT

1 full side of salmon, about 5 pounds, bones removed and skin on

3 tablespoons olive oil, divided

2 teaspoons Aromatic Salt (see below)

1 lemon, cut into thin rounds, and then the rounds cut in half

AROMATIC SALT

2 cups fine sea salt

1 cup finely chopped fresh herbs (mixture of rosemary, sage, thyme, and parsley)

1 lemon for zesting

Place salmon on a cutting board and trim off the fatty belly portion and pull pin bones.

Slice salmon into portions approximately 2–3 inches wide, down to the skin, but not through the skin.

Place the fillet on a sheet pan that has been coated with 2 tablespoons oil. Tuck narrow tail end under and spread remaining oil on top of the fillet. Sprinkle with the Aromatic Salt and spread it evenly over fillet. Tuck 2 lemon slices into each cut and place in the oven. Roast for 18–20 minutes, rotating the pan every 6 minutes or so. An instant-read thermometer should read around 120°F. Let the salmon rest for 5 minutes before serving.

To serve, use a fish spatula and scoop between the skin and the fish to remove from the sheet pan. The entire length of the skin should remain on the pan.

Aromatic Salt

Put the salt-and-herb mixture onto sheet pan and toss together. Hold the lemon over salt mixture and zest. Toss again to combine well. Aromatic Salt can be used immediately or left out at room temperature to dry for 48 hours, then kept in the refrigerator for future use.

SERVES 6–8

Pesce al Forno

Reserve this recipe for smaller intimate dining, as a whole fish often yields a fairly small amount once cooked and the bones removed. This is a beautiful and colorful Mediterranean-style presentation for your table.

ROASTING OVEN ENVIRONMENT

1$\frac{1}{2}$ pounds unpeeled Yukon gold potatoes, cut in 1-inch dice
2 teaspoons sea salt, divided
2 teaspoons chopped fresh thyme
$\frac{1}{3}$ cup plus 2 tablespoons olive oil
Roasted Cherry Tomatoes (see below)
8 anchovy fillets, in oil, drained
6 cloves garlic, thinly sliced
2 roasted red peppers, sliced*
1 whole fish, about 3$\frac{1}{2}$–4 pounds (sea bass, cod, etc.), head on and scaled
Pepper

ROASTED CHERRY TOMATOES

1 basket small cherry tomatoes, rinsed
3 tablespoons extra virgin olive oil
$\frac{1}{2}$ teaspoon kosher salt

In the bottom of a roasting pan large enough to hold the fish, add the potatoes and toss with 1 teaspoon salt, thyme, and $\frac{1}{3}$ cup oil. Place in the oven and roast for about 10 minutes, or until the potatoes have begun to soften. Add Roasted Cherry Tomatoes, garlic, anchovies, and roasted peppers; cook for 5 minutes more.

While the vegetables are roasting, rinse and dry the fish and place it on a cutting board. Make three "X" slashes through the skin on each side of the fish. Season with the remaining salt, pepper, and remaining oil. Rub the fish inside and out.

Place the fish on top of the vegetables and roast for 20–30 minutes more, or until the fish registers 125ºF on an instant-read thermometer in the thickest part. Let rest for 5 minutes before serving.

Roasted Cherry Tomatoes

Place the tomatoes on a sheet pan with oil. Toss to coat and set in the oven. Cook until slightly charred and softened, about 5 minutes. Remove, add salt, and set aside.

*To roast the peppers, place on a sheet pan and set in the oven during the perimeter burn of oven startup. Blacken skin on peppers, turning once or twice to evenly char. Do not overcook or peppers will dehydrate. Peppers should be blackened on the outside with a tender and juicy interior. Remove from oven, place in a bowl, and let rest, uncovered, until cool enough to touch. Once cool, remove the charred skin and the seeds. Do not rinse with water.

SERVES 4

Sautéed Fillet of Petrale Sole

Combine the freshest fish with the highest heat and you have the finest results—crisp exterior with the fresh saltwater flavor of tender fish fillets.

ROASTING OVEN ENVIRONMENT

4 sole fillets, about 4 ounces each
1/4 cup all-purpose flour
1/2 teaspoon salt
2 tablespoons olive oil

Lightly dredge the fish in the flour, shaking off any excess. Season with salt.

Heat a sauté pan (that is large enough to hold the fish in a single layer) for 5 minutes in the oven. Add the oil and heat for another 30 seconds.

Hold the fish so just the tip of the fillet touches the pan. If it doesn't sizzle, return the pan to the oven and heat for another minute or so. It is very important to have a very hot pan so the fish won't stick.

When the pan is hot, add the fish and cook for 2 minutes on each side. The sole will just start to brown on the edges and should flake easily when done.

SERVES 4

POULTRY

Perfectly Roasted Whole Chicken

One of the most frequently asked questions we receive at Mugnaini is how to roast a chicken. There is nothing more delicious than a juicy, succulent, well-seasoned, perfectly roasted chicken! I am always pleased to say how easy this is to achieve in the moist, high heat of a wood-burning oven.

ROASTING OVEN ENVIRONMENT

1 whole chicken, about 4½ to 5 pounds
2 tablespoons Compound Butter, softened
    (see below)
1 teaspoon salt, divided
1 (3-inch) sprig each fresh thyme, sage,
    and rosemary
Butcher's twine

COMPOUND BUTTER

1 stick unsalted butter, softened
1 small clove garlic, minced
2 teaspoons chopped fresh thyme
1 teaspoon chopped parsley
½ teaspoon orange zest

Rinse chicken with cold water and pat dry.

Gently loosen the skin on the breast with your finger. Place 1 tablespoon Compound Butter under the skin on each side of chicken. Spread as evenly as possible. Sprinkle about ¼ teaspoon salt inside the cavity of the chicken and add the sprigs of herbs. Tie the legs together with the twine. Rub remaining salt on the outside of the chicken.

Place chicken on its side on a "V" rack in a roasting pan and loosely tent with foil. Place into the oven so the back of the chicken is towards the flame and the legs are towards the rear of the oven. Cook for about 15 minutes. Remove pan from oven and carefully turn the chicken breast side up. Continue cooking and rotating pan so the chicken browns evenly. Keep the chicken tented during roasting time. Check for doneness at 45 minutes and cook for about 30 minutes more, or until an instant-read thermometer registers 165°F when inserted where the thigh attaches to the body. Be sure to check the temperature in both thighs. Remove and let rest for 15 minutes before carving.

Compound Butter

Combine all of the ingredients together in a small bowl. Leftover butter can be rolled into a log, wrapped, and frozen for up to 3 months.

SERVES 4

Vertical Roasted Chicken

This is another deliciously simple roasted chicken recipe for those who use vertical roasting racks. If roasting more than one bird at a time, it is easier to place each chicken on its own quarter sheet pan.

ROASTING OVEN ENVIRONMENT

2½ teaspoons kosher salt, divided
1 whole chicken, about 4½ to 5 pounds

Sprinkle 1 teaspoon salt into the cavity of the chicken. Rub remaining salt on the exterior.

Tuck the wings behind the chicken and wrap the tips with foil.

Place the vertical roaster in the center of a sheet pan. Set the chicken down over the top, so the tip of the legs actually touch the pan. Place in the oven. Start with the back towards the flame and brown. Turn the sheet pan a quarter turn as each side browns for a total of 50–60 minutes. If the top browns excessively, cover with a small piece of foil. Chicken is done when the area where the thigh attaches to the body reaches 165°F. Be sure to check the temperature in both thighs. Remove from the oven and allow to rest 10–15 minutes before carving.

SERVES 4

Butterflied Chicken with Sage Pesto

A butterflied chicken roasts faster than a whole bird. This recipe is always a crowd pleaser because the skin is crisp, the meat stays moist, and it is well seasoned by the herb paste tucked under the skin.

ROASTING OVEN ENVIRONMENT

1 whole chicken, about 4 pounds
1 bunch fresh sage, about 6–8 whole leaves
2 sprigs fresh parsley
3 cloves garlic
2 teaspoons salt
1 teaspoon freshly ground black pepper
Extra virgin olive oil

On a cutting board, stand the chicken, neck end up, with the back facing towards you. With a sharp boning knife, cut down through both sides of the spine and remove.

Open the chicken skin side up and press down firmly with the heel of your hand to flatten.

Place the sage, parsley, and garlic on the cutting board or in a food processor and finely chop. Place in a small bowl and add the salt and pepper. Drizzle in the oil and stir until the mixture has a paste-like texture.

Gently loosen the skin on breasts and legs with your fingers. Using a teaspoon, spread the herb paste under the skin as evenly as possible over the meat of both breasts and legs.

Place chicken on a rack set in a roasting pan and place in the oven. Tent loosely with foil and rotate as chicken browns. Check the temperature in both thighs after 20 minutes and rotate the pan as needed to achieve even cooking. Continue to cook, checking temperature, until each thigh registers 165°F, about 30–45 minutes. Remove from oven, cover, and let rest for 10 minutes before carving.

SERVES 4

Stuffed Chicken Breasts

This pan-seared recipe is another example of how to use your oven floor as a cooktop. A hot pan and hot oil ensure a well-seared chicken breast bursting with a moist textured stuffing. For an elegant presentation, slice to serve.

ROASTING OVEN ENVIRONMENT

2 teaspoons olive oil
1/4 pound sliced pancetta, finely chopped
1 tablespoon finely chopped shallot
1 tablespoon dried currants
2 tablespoons chopped toasted pine nuts
1 tablespoon grated Parmigiano-Reggiano cheese
1/4 cup grated Asiago cheese
1 tablespoon chopped fresh parsley
4 boneless chicken breasts, about 6 ounces each
1 teaspoon salt
1/2 teaspoon freshly ground pepper
2–4 tablespoons extra virgin olive oil

Heat oil in a small sauté pan over medium-high heat. Add the pancetta and cook until it begins to render its fat. Add the shallot and continue cooking until softened and the pancetta begins to brown, about 4 minutes. Place shallot and pancetta in a medium bowl and add the currants; stir to combine and let cool. When the mixture is cooled, add the pine nuts, cheeses, and parsley.

Place a chicken breast on a cutting board. With a paring knife, cut a small slit into the side of the breast, running the knife parallel to the cutting board. Be careful not to cut through the bottom or the opposite side of the breast. You have now created a pocket to hold the filling. Place 2 tablespoons of the filling in the pocket. Do not overstuff or you will lose the filling as the chicken cooks. Repeat process with the remaining chicken breasts. Lightly season both sides with salt and pepper.

Place a large sauté pan in the oven for 5 minutes to heat. Remove and add 2 tablespoons oil. Return the pan to the oven and heat for 30 seconds more. Once the oil is hot, add the chicken in a single layer, skin side down. Cook, uncovered, for 5 minutes. When the chicken is nicely browned and releases easily from the pan, flip over and cook for 4–5 minutes more, adding more oil if necessary. Remove from the oven, cover loosely with foil, and let rest 5 minutes before serving.

SERVES 4

Chicken Cutlets with Cherry Tomatoes and Basil

This fast-cooking recipe is best during the summer when tomatoes and basil are fresh and most flavorful. Due to the short cooking time, be sure to have all the ingredients prepared before you start.

ROASTING OVEN ENVIRONMENT

4 boneless, skinless chicken breasts, about 6 ounces each

2 teaspoons salt, divided

½ cup all-purpose flour

1 to 2 tablespoons olive oil

2 shallots, chopped

1 clove garlic, chopped

1 basket cherry tomatoes

¼ cup dry white wine

1 tablespoon capers

¼ cup chopped basil

3 tablespoons cream

Place chicken breasts between two sheets of plastic and pound until ¼ inch thick. Season cutlets with 1½ teaspoons salt and then lightly dredge with flour, shaking off any excess.

Place a sauté pan large enough to hold two cutlets in the oven; heat for 5 minutes. Add 1 tablespoon oil and then heat for 30 seconds more.

Place the chicken cutlets in the pan in a single layer. Turn the chicken when it is lightly browned, about 4 minutes. Cook for about 4 minutes more. Remove to a plate, cover, and set aside in a warm place. Cook the remaining chicken, adding more oil to the pan if necessary.

In the now empty sauté pan, add the shallots, garlic, and tomatoes. Cook for about 3 minutes, or until the tomatoes begin to burst. Add the wine and capers and cook for 2 minutes more. Stir in the basil and cream.

To serve, place chicken on a serving platter and pour the sauce over the top.

SERVES 4

Chicken Cacciatore

Many families have their own chicken cacciatore recipe that has been handed down for generations. The Mugnaini family version includes a little red chile, citrus, and sweet wood-roasted peppers. This version allows you to perform every step of the recipe in a wood-fired oven.

ROASTING OVEN ENVIRONMENT

1 (4-pound) whole fryer, cut into 8 pieces

2 teaspoons salt

½ teaspoon freshly ground pepper

¼ cup olive oil

1 onion, quartered then thinly sliced

3 cloves garlic, sliced

½ teaspoon red chile flakes

2 teaspoons chopped fresh rosemary

1 cup dry white wine

1 cup canned crushed San Marzano or other
     good-quality tomatoes

1 cup chicken stock

½ cup whole green olives

2 tablespoons orange zest, divided

1 each red and yellow bell pepper, roasted and
     cut into 1-inch strips (to roast, see page 68)

1 tablespoon chopped parsley

Rinse the chicken with cold water and pat dry with paper towels. Season with salt and pepper; set aside.

Place a sauté pan large enough to hold the chicken in a single layer in the oven. Heat for 1–2 minutes, add the oil, and then heat for 30 seconds more. Add the chicken skin side down and cook for about 8–10 minutes, or until brown. Turn and cook for about 5 minutes more. Remove chicken to a plate, cover, and set aside.

Pour out all but 2 tablespoons oil from the sauté pan and add the onion, garlic, chile flakes, and rosemary. Place back into the oven and cook until the onion softens, being careful not to burn the garlic, about 4 minutes. Add the wine and continue to cook until the wine reduces to about ½ cup, about 4 minutes more.

Remove the sauté pan from the oven and add the tomatoes, stock, olives, 1 tablespoon orange zest, and roasted peppers. Stir to combine and add the chicken back to the pan, along with any accumulated juices. Cover and return to the oven for about 30 minutes, or until the chicken is tender and the thighs reach an internal temperature of 165°F. Garnish with the parsley and remaining orange zest.

SERVES 6–8 AS AN APPETIZER OR 4 AS A FIRST PLATE

Braised Pheasant Tuscan Style

During our fall cooking classes in Tuscany, the pheasants are brought to our kitchen fresh from the field, feathers and all. This recipe is from Carla, my cooking assistant in Tuscany, who is one of the best home chefs I have ever met.

ROASTING OVEN ENVIRONMENT

2 pheasants (may substitute chicken)
1 tablespoon salt
1 teaspoon pepper
¼ cup olive oil
1 red onion, medium dice
2 stalks celery, medium dice
2 carrots, medium dice
1 cup Vin Santo
1 (14-ounce) can whole San Marzano or other
    good-quality tomatoes
¼ cup whole oil-cured black olives
2–2½ cups low-sodium chicken stock
2 tablespoons chopped parsley

Remove the backbone from each pheasant. Cut each pheasant into 4 pieces (leg and thigh combination, and 2 half breasts). Rinse and dry thoroughly, then season with salt and pepper.

Place roasting pan in oven and heat for 5 minutes. Add the oil and then heat for 30 seconds more. Add the pheasant pieces and brown on both sides, about 20 minutes, turning once. Remove the pheasant to a plate and cover.

Add the onion, celery, and carrots to the pan. Cook for about 10–12 minutes, or until the vegetables are softened and lightly browned. Add the Vin Santo and cook until partially evaporated, about 2 minutes. Add the tomatoes and olives and heat through, about 2 minutes.

Place the pheasant and any accumulated juices back into the pan and add enough stock to cover by one-third. Cover tightly and cook for 2 hours, or until the pheasant is tender and falls easily from the bone. Check occasionally to make sure there is enough liquid, adding more stock if necessary. Remove from oven and adjust seasoning with salt and pepper. Garnish with parsley.

SERVES 6–8

Thanksgiving Turkey

All Americans want to be successful with their Thanksgiving turkey. Study this recipe and practice well before time—maybe even in July! When the big day comes, be sure to record internal temperatures, rotate the pan, and maintain the pan juices for delicious gravy.

ROASTING OVEN ENVIRONMENT

1 whole turkey, about 20 pounds
2 tablespoons Compound Butter (page 72)
2½ teaspoons salt, divided
1 teaspoon freshly ground pepper
1 bunch fresh thyme sprigs, left whole
2 cloves garlic, halved
1 unpeeled orange, cut into four sections
1 tablespoon extra virgin olive oil
2 stalks celery, coarsely chopped
1 white onion, coarsely chopped
1 cup water, more if needed

Wash the turkey with cold water and pat dry with paper towels inside and outside. Slide your hand under the skin on the turkey breasts and loosen skin from meat. Rub half of the butter on each side. Season inside of turkey with 2 teaspoons salt and the pepper, and then stuff with thyme, garlic, and orange sections. Tie the turkey legs together. Rub olive oil over outside of turkey and sprinkle with remaining salt. Set turkey on its side on a "V" roasting rack set in a roasting pan.

Place the celery, onion, and water on bottom of roasting pan. Place a heavy-duty foil tent over turkey and set in the oven with the back side facing the fire and the legs toward the rear of the oven. Leave in this position for 45 minutes. Remove turkey from oven and turn breast side up in roasting pan. Insert an internal thermometer into both hip joints and begin to record temperatures. Add water to pan to keep bottom covered with liquid if necessary. Replace foil tent over turkey and set back in the oven with the lesser cooked side positioned towards the fire. Repeat internal temperature checks every 30 minutes and rotate pan, positioning lesser cooked side of turkey towards the fire. Baste turkey during temperature checks if needed. Continue to roast until internal temperature at each hip joint registers 165°F. Total roasting time is usually 3 hours.

SERVES 10–12

Mediterranean Braised Chicken with Meyer Lemon and Fennel

A Mugnaini class favorite! This braised chicken starts by getting browned with a large flame for extra flavor and finishes in a stock of aromatic vegetables and sweet Meyer lemon—superb for entertaining.

ROASTING OVEN ENVIRONMENT

6 pounds chicken legs and thighs

1 teaspoon sea salt

½ teaspoon freshly ground black pepper

2 tablespoons all-purpose flour

3 tablespoons extra virgin olive oil

3 cloves garlic, sliced

2 teaspoons chopped rosemary

2 cups dry white wine

2 bulbs fennel, cut into wedges and fronds reserved

3 Meyer lemons, sliced into rounds and seeds removed

1¼ cups large whole green olives (Cerignola)

½ cup chicken stock, plus more if necessary

¼ cup chopped flat-leaf parsley

1 Meyer lemon, zested (about 1 tablespoon)

¼ cup chopped fennel fronds (from reserved above)

Rinse and pat the chicken dry. Place in a bowl and sprinkle with salt, pepper, and flour; toss to coat.

Place a pan large enough to hold the chicken in a single layer in the oven (a large paella pan works well) and heat for 5 minutes. Add the oil and then heat for 30 seconds more.

Add the chicken to the pan skin side down and cook until the bottom has browned, about 10–15 minutes. Turn the chicken and then add the garlic, rosemary, and wine and cook to reduce the wine by half, about 15–20 minutes. Add the fennel, lemon slices, olives, and stock and tightly cover. Cook for 45–60 minutes, checking occasionally to make sure there is enough liquid. Add more chicken stock if necessary. Chicken should be fork tender. Remove from the oven and add the parsley, zest, and fennel fronds.

SERVES 6–8

Citrus-Marinated Grilled Chicken Breasts with Mango Relish

We have been using this recipe for years to demonstrate the grilling technique in a pizza oven. The citrus and olive oil marinade and the hot coals ensure a juicy, tender chicken breast every time.

OVEN GRILLING ENVIRONMENT

4 boneless, skinless chicken breasts,
   about 6 ounces each
Juice from 1 orange
Juice from 1/2 lemon
1 teaspoon salt
1/2 teaspoon freshly ground black pepper
1 tablespoon extra virgin olive oil
Mango Cucumber Relish (see below)

MANGO CUCUMBER RELISH

1 mango, peeled and diced 1/4 inch
1 small red bell pepper, diced 1/4 inch
1 English cucumber, unpeeled and diced 1/4 inch
1 small red onion, finely chopped
1 small jalapeño, finely chopped with ribs and
   seeds removed
1 tablespoon extra virgin olive oil
1/4 cup chopped fresh cilantro
1/4 cup fresh Key lime juice
Pinch of ground cumin
Salt to taste

Rinse the chicken breasts with cold water and pat dry. Place between two sheets of plastic and pound lightly to a uniform thickness of about 1/2 inch. Place chicken breasts in a shallow bowl or ziplock bag with all remaining ingredients except Relish and mix well. Place in the refrigerator to marinate for 1–2 hours. Remove from refrigerator 30 minutes before grilling, leaving in marinade.

Position hot coals forward in the oven to prepare for grilling. Oil a Mugnaini Tuscan Grill, set over coals, and heat for 5 minutes to heat well. Place chicken breasts on grill and cook for 2 minutes on each side. Do not overcook. Remove, cover with foil, and let rest for 10 minutes before slicing.

To serve, thinly slice on the diagonal and top with the Mango Cucumber Relish.

Mango Cucumber Relish
Combine all ingredients except salt in a mixing bowl and combine well. Add salt to taste.

SERVES 4–6

Chicken Piccata

This recipe is another classic that benefits from cooking quickly in a hot pizza oven. Be sure to have all of the ingredients measured and ready to assemble before starting.

PIZZA OVEN ENVIRONMENT

4 boneless, skinless chicken breasts,
    about 6 ounces each
1$\frac{1}{2}$ teaspoons salt
$\frac{1}{2}$ cup all-purpose flour
1–2 tablespoons oil
1 clove garlic, chopped
$\frac{1}{2}$ cup dry white wine
$\frac{1}{2}$ cup chicken broth
1 tablespoon fresh lemon juice
2 tablespoons capers
2 tablespoons unsalted butter
1 tablespoon chopped parsley

Place chicken breasts between two sheets of plastic and pound until $\frac{1}{4}$ inch thick. Season with salt and then lightly dredge with flour, shaking off any excess.

Place a sauté pan large enough for two cutlets in the oven; heat for 5 minutes. Add 1 tablespoon oil and then heat for 30 seconds more.

Place the cutlets in a single layer in the hot sauté pan. Turn the chicken when it is lightly browned, about 4 minutes. Cook about 4 minutes more. Remove to a plate, cover, and set aside. Continue with the remaining chicken, adding more oil to the pan if necessary.

In the now empty sauté pan, add the garlic and deglaze with the wine. Cook for about 3 minutes, or until the wine has reduced to 2 tablespoons, being careful not to burn the garlic. Add the broth, lemon juice, capers, and chicken cutlets. Cook for 1–2 minutes. Place chicken on serving plates. Add the butter and parsley to sauté pan, swirl to combine, and then pour over chicken.

SERVES 4–6

Chicken under a Brick

This chicken is the single most favorite chicken recipe in our cooking classes. Ask your butcher to debone a chicken per the recipe, or follow the instructions below. Deboning ensures the breast meat and leg meat will cook evenly and simultaneously. It also allows for beautiful slices and easy carving at the table.

ROASTING OVEN ENVIRONMENT

1 chicken, about 4 pounds, left whole, bones removed except for the wings and knuckle ends of drumsticks (see note)

1 teaspoon Aromatic Salt (page 66), divided

2 tablespoons extra virgin olive oil

2 heavy bricks wrapped with foil

½ lemon

Cut chicken through the center of the breast so chicken is in two halves. Sprinkle ¼ teaspoon Aromatic Salt on the back of each half. Turn chicken over and, with your fingers, gently loosen the skin on each breast. Place ¼ teaspoon salt under the skin of each half. Rub 1 tablespoon oil over the skin of each half.

Place sheet pan in oven for at least 5 minutes to heat well. Slide pan towards oven opening and carefully place chicken skin side down on pan. Immediately place bricks on top of chicken, covering as much of the chicken as possible. Place pan back in the oven and cook for 12 minutes, or until the skin side is nicely browned. Remove sheet pan from oven and lift off bricks. Return to oven and cook, uncovered, for 6–8 minutes more, or until the thigh temperatures read 165°F. Remove from oven and allow to rest for 5 minutes before carving. Squeeze lemon over chicken before serving.

SERVES 4

NOTE FROM THE AUTHOR: To bone a chicken, stand chicken upright with neck end at top and back facing you. Grip firmly with one hand and, using a sharp boning knife, cut down through both sides of the spine and remove it. Set chicken, breast side down, on a work surface and cut flesh along both sides of the rib cage, staying as close to the bone as possible, being careful at all times not to puncture the skin. Cut through the joint where the rib cage is attached to the wing and remove the saber bone. Cut through the joint where the thigh connects to the spine. Gently pull entire rib cage free from the chicken. Lay the chicken open, skin side down, on a work surface. Feel for the thigh bone and slice into the meat to expose the bone. Scrape meat from the thigh bone, working your way over the knee, and scrape meat two-thirds of the way down the drumstick. Using the back of your knife, crack the bone at this point and remove, leaving only the knuckle end of the drumstick. Repeat on opposite side.

MEAT

Braised Short Ribs with Orange-Spiced Red Wine

These short ribs receive extra flavor from the deep browning resulting from the high heat from the flame and the slow roasting for hours in the fennel and citrus-spiced wine.

LARGE BROWNING FLAME TRANSITIONING TO ROASTING OVEN ENVIRONMENT

GREMOLATA
1 tablespoon grated lemon zest
1 clove garlic, finely chopped
¼ cup finely chopped parsley

RIBS
6 short ribs, about 5 pounds
3½ cups red wine, such as Zinfandel
8 allspice berries
10 whole cloves
3 cloves garlic, crushed
1 teaspoon fennel seeds, crushed
1 tablespoon orange zest
1 tablespoon salt (if using commercial beef stock, omit salt from recipe)
½ teaspoon freshly ground black pepper
2 tablespoons olive oil
1 yellow onion, roughly chopped
2 carrots, peeled and roughly chopped
3 stalks celery, roughly chopped
4–6 cups beef stock, divided
3 sprigs rosemary, about 4 inches each
2 sprigs fresh sage
3 bay leaves

SAUCE
Braising liquid
Beef stock, if necessary
2 teaspoons good-quality balsamic vinegar
2 tablespoons fresh orange juice
Salt and pepper, to taste

Mix the gremolata ingredients together and place on a plate or piece of parchment. Leave out on counter to air dry.

Place the ribs, wine, allspice, cloves, garlic, fennel, and orange zest in shallow dish or ziplock bag. Cover and refrigerate for 24 hours. Remove ribs from the marinade, reserve marinade, pat ribs dry with paper towels, and season on all sides with salt and pepper.

Place a roasting pan large enough to hold the ribs in a single layer in the oven and heat 5 minutes. Add the oil and then heat for 30 seconds more. Add the ribs and sear, turning until brown on all sides, about 10–12 minutes. Remove from pan and set aside. Add the onion, carrots, and celery to pan and cook for 5–6 minutes, or until softened. While vegetables are cooking, strain the reserved marinade through a fine sieve and pour into a liquid measuring cup. You should have 3 cups; if not, add wine. Pour into the roasting pan, return to oven, and cook until reduced by one-third, about 5 minutes. Add 2 cups beef stock and heat. Add ribs and any accumulated juices back to pan along with the rosemary, sage, and bay leaves. Cover and cook in oven for about 3 hours, checking liquid level and adding more broth as needed to keep one-third of the beef covered, and turning ribs about every 30 minutes. Meat should fall easily from the bone when done.

continued on page 94

Remove ribs and place on a platter, tightly covered, and hold in a 200°F oven while you make the sauce.

Sauce

Pour braising liquid into a gravy separator or gently spoon off fat from the top. Carefully decant the liquid without the fat into a liquid measuring cup. You should have about 2 cups; if less, add beef stock. Pour into saucepan, bring to a boil, and reduce heat to medium high. Cook until reduced by half. Scrape down the sides of the pan frequently while the liquid is reducing. Turn the heat to low and add the vinegar and orange juice. Heat through, then taste for seasonings. Pour sauce over the ribs and sprinkle with the gremolata. Serve immediately.

SERVES 4

Standing Rib Roast

This roast will beautifully sear in the moist, high heat of the oven, creating a crisp, flavorful exterior while maintaining a moist, juicy interior. Follow these instructions for a well-seasoned, succulent roast that is also very easy to carve.

 LARGE BROWNING FLAME TRANSITIONING TO ROASTING OVEN ENVIRONMENT

1 bone-in beef rib roast, about 19–20 pounds
2 tablespoons chopped rosemary
4 tablespoons kosher salt, divided
1 teaspoon pepper
1 tablespoon chopped garlic

If refrigerator space is available, place roast, uncovered, on a rack over a sheet pan and allow to "air dry" for 3 days. Remove roast 2 hours before roasting.

Mix the rosemary, 1 tablespoon salt, pepper, and garlic together in a small bowl; set aside.

Using a sharp knife, slice the bones away from the roast about three-fourths of the way down, creating a pocket. Rub the rosemary mixture into the pocket. With butcher's twine, tie the bones back to the roast between each rib. Rub the remaining salt all over the roast. Place the rib roast on its side on a "V" rack in a roasting pan and then tent with foil. Roast for 30 minutes with the ribs closest to the fire. Remove pan from oven and carefully roll the roast so the fat side is up. Return to the oven and roast, rotating the pan every 30 minutes for about 3½ hours, or until the internal temperature in the center of the roast reaches 120°F. Remove from the oven and let rest 30 minutes, covered. (Larger cuts of meat need more resting time to redistribute their juices, and the internal temperature will increase more than a smaller cut of meat.) To serve, remove the bones from the roast and slice.

SERVES 14–15

Tuscan-Style Pot Roast with Herbs and Chianti

The flavorful balance of herbs and spice with a rich reduction of wine transforms the humble pot roast into something special. Enjoy with oven-roasted potatoes.

LARGE BROWNING FLAME TRANSITIONING TO ROASTING OVEN ENVIRONMENT

1 (1/2-inch-thick) slice pancetta

2 cloves garlic

2 tablespoons rosemary leaves

6 fresh sage leaves plus 1 sprig sage

1 teaspoon salt

1/2 teaspoon freshly ground pepper

1 (3–4 pound) boneless beef chuck roast, rolled and tied

2 tablespoons extra virgin olive oil

1 large red onion (or 2 medium), coarsely chopped

2 stalks celery, coarsely chopped

3 carrots, coarsely chopped

5 whole allspice berries

2 tablespoons tomato paste

3 1/2 cups Chianti wine

4 cups canned whole San Marzano tomatoes, with juices

2 sprigs fresh parsley, with stem

Place the pancetta, garlic, rosemary, sage leaves, salt, and pepper in the bowl of a food processor fitted with a metal blade and chop until fine and almost paste-like in texture. Rub herb mixture over roast, pushing into the folds of the meat.

Place a large heavy-bottom saucepan in the oven and heat for 5 minutes. Add oil and heat for 30 seconds more. Add roast and brown on all sides, turning as necessary. Add the onion, celery, carrots, sage sprig, and allspice to pan. Cook until vegetables are lightly browned and softened. Add the tomato paste and cook, stirring well, until heated through and fragrant. Add the wine and cook for about 2 minutes. Add the tomatoes and parsley, cover the pan, and cook for about 2–2 1/2 hours, or until fork tender. Remove roast from pan. Strain pan juices and season with salt and pepper to taste. Serve roast with the sauce.

SERVES 6–8

Classic Bistecca alla Fiorentina

Try this classic Florentine style for grilling your next steak. Plan in advance and ask your meat vendor for this special thicker cut of beef.

GRILLING ENVIRONMENT

Well-aged T-bone or porterhouse steak, cut between 2–3 inches thick
Coarse sea salt
Extra virgin olive oil
Freshly ground black pepper

Try to purchase the steak at least 3 days before grilling, and place it on a flat roasting rack set on a quarter sheet pan and keep uncovered in your refrigerator. Remove from refrigerator 30 minutes before grilling.

Heat grill well for 5 minutes. Place steak onto grill with bone portion towards the rear of grill and cook for about 3–5 minutes. Turn steak over and cook second side for 3–5 minutes more. Set steak up on flat bone end and cook for 1 minute. Meat should be seared and crisp on exterior and red, almost raw, at the very center at bone section. Remove, salt well, and let rest for 5 minutes before serving.

To serve, carve meat from the bone and slice for each portion. Drizzle with oil and serve with additional salt and freshly ground pepper to taste.

SERVES 2–3

Wood-Roasted Whole Beef Tenderloin in Aromatic Salt

This is an easy way to serve a large luxurious cut of meat. Obtain the best-quality product and follow these instructions, especially the post-roasting rest period, for results that will yield meat cooked in a range to please everyone's taste.

LARGE BROWNING FLAME TRANSITIONING TO ROASTING OVEN ENVIRONMENT

1 trimmed whole beef tenderloin, about 3½ pounds
Butcher's twine
1 tablespoon Aromatic Salt (page 66)
1 teaspoon freshly ground black pepper
2 tablespoons olive oil

Place the tenderloin on a cutting board. Turn the small, narrow tail-end of the tenderloin under to help create an equal thickness. Using the butcher's twine, tie the entire length of the tenderloin in 1- to 1½-inch intervals. (The goal is to create even cooking time throughout the roast by having the thickness as equal as possible from end to end.) Pat the tenderloin dry and season with the Aromatic Salt and pepper.

Place a half sheet pan in the oven and heat for 5 minutes. Add the oil and heat for 30 seconds more. Place the tenderloin on the hot sheet pan and return to the oven.

Using tongs, roll the tenderloin and brown evenly. Continue roasting for about 20–25 minutes, checking the temperature every 5 minutes, until the internal temperature of the middle section of the tenderloin reaches 120°F. This will allow for a range of doneness—rare in the midsection progressing to well-done on the ends. Remove from oven, cover, and allow to rest for 10 minutes.

SERVES 6–8

Osso Bucco

A classic recipe that many of you have probably enjoyed for years. Now you can cook this in your wood-burning oven, performing every step from the initial browning to the long, slow braise.

LARGE BROWNING FLAME TRANSITIONING TO ROASTING OVEN ENVIRONMENT

6 pounds veal shanks, sliced crosswise into
    2-inch pieces
½ cup all-purpose flour
2 teaspoons kosher salt
½ teaspoon freshly ground pepper
2 tablespoons olive oil
¼ pound thickly cut pancetta, cut in ½-inch dice
3 leeks, cleaned and sliced, about 3 cups
1 bulb fennel, cut in ½ inch dice
    (fronds reserved)
2 cloves garlic, sliced
2 carrots, cut in ½ inch dice
1 tablespoon tomato paste
1 (14.5-ounce) can San Marzano or other good-
    quality tomatoes, drained and crushed
1 sprig rosemary, about 4 inches long
2 sprigs thyme
2 bay leaves
3 strips orange zest, about 1 x 4 inches each
4 cups chicken, beef, or veal stock, divided
1 cup Cabernet Sauvignon or other red wine

Dredge the shanks in the flour, shake off excess, and season with the salt and pepper.

Place a pan large enough to hold the shanks in one layer in the oven. Heat pan for 5 minutes, add the oil, and then heat for 30 seconds more. Add the shanks and brown, turning once, for about 15 minutes. Remove from the pan and set aside.

Add the pancetta to the pan and cook until lightly browned, about 4 minutes. Add the leeks, fennel, garlic, carrots, and tomato paste and cook until tender, about 8 minutes. Stir in the tomatoes, rosemary, thyme, bay leaves, orange zest, 2 cups stock, and wine. Heat for about 3 minutes.

Add the shanks plus any accumulated juices back to the pan, nestling into the vegetables and liquid. Cover tightly and cook for about 1½ hours, or until fork tender. Check the liquid level in the pan a few times during cooking to be sure it remains one-third of the way up the shanks. Add more stock if needed. Remove from the oven, taste for seasoning, and sprinkle with 2 tablespoons chopped reserved fennel fronds.

SERVES 6

Roasted Boneless Leg of Lamb with Rosemary and Garlic

More than any other meat, I love the way lamb responds to the high heat during searing in the oven. The meat takes on a sweet, aromatic characteristic as it cooks with the particular seasonings of each recipe and, in this case, the simple savory blend of rosemary and garlic.

LARGE BROWNING FLAME TRANSITIONING TO ROASTING OVEN ENVIRONMENT

1 tablespoon chopped rosemary
1 tablespoon plus 2 teaspoons kosher salt, divided
1 tablespoon chopped garlic
1 (7–8-pound) boneless leg of lamb
¼ teaspoon freshly ground black pepper

In a small bowl, mix together the rosemary, 1 tablespoon salt, and garlic.

If the lamb has an elastic "sock" on it, gently remove. Unfold the lamb and rub the rosemary mixture on the underside (not the fat side). Gather the lamb back together in its original shape and place the sock back on, or tie with butcher's twine at 2-inch increments.

Rub the outside of the lamb with the remaining salt and pepper.

Place the lamb on a "V" rack in a roasting pan so it is on its side, and tent the pan with aluminum foil. Place in the oven so the underside is next to the flame and the fat side is farthest away.

Roast for 30 minutes and then gently turn the lamb so the fat side is up. Continue to cook, rotating pan every 30 minutes, for another 2–2½ hours, or until an internal temperature of 135ºF for medium has been reached. Remove from the oven and let rest, covered, for 20 minutes.

SERVES 12–14

Butterflied Leg of Lamb with Pecorino Cheese

This may sound like an unusual combination, but don't be intimidated by the anchovies and pecorino. Together, their flavors are highly compatible with lamb and meld in the dish to create the final uniquely special flavor.

LARGE BROWNING FLAME TRANSITIONING TO ROASTING OVEN ENVIRONMENT

1 (7–8-pound) boneless, butterflied leg of lamb (remove lamb from the refrigerator at oven firing time)

2 teaspoons salt

1 teaspoon pepper

1 tablespoon chopped rosemary

1 (2-ounce) can anchovies in oil

3 large cloves garlic

¼ cup olive oil

1 cup dry white wine

1½ cups chicken stock, divided

¾ cup grated pecorino cheese

Place the lamb on a work surface. Cut off any large clumps of fat. Season with salt and pepper.

Place the rosemary in a small bowl. Chop the anchovies and garlic together and then add to rosemary; set aside.

Place a roasting pan large enough to hold the lamb in one layer in the oven. Heat for 5 minutes, add the oil, and heat for 30 seconds more.

Place lamb in pan, fat side down, and brown, turning once, for about 12–15 minutes.

Add garlic mixture to the pan and cook for 1–2 minutes, being careful not to burn. Add the wine and ½ cup stock; stir to combine. Continue roasting meat, rotating the pan and checking the level of liquid in the bottom of the pan. After 20 minutes, add the remaining stock if you haven't done so already. Cook until the meat in the thickest part reaches an internal temperature of 135°F for medium, about 45–50 minutes.

Sprinkle cheese on lamb and return to oven for 2 minutes, or until the cheese browns and bubbles. Remove from oven, cover, and let rest for 20 minutes. Pour pan juices through a fat separator; keep warm and serve with roast.

SERVES 10–12

Braised Lamb Shanks al Forno

This recipe has been popular for years in our wood-fired cooking classes. The pan searing in the oven followed by slow cooking in plenty of liquid produces a fork-tender texture from an otherwise tough cut of meat. Don't rush—give yourself plenty of time for the best results.

LARGE BROWNING FLAME TRANSITIONING TO ROASTING OVEN ENVIRONMENT

6 lamb shanks, cracked, about 8 pounds
1 teaspoon kosher salt
1/2 teaspoon freshly ground black pepper
1 tablespoon sliced garlic
1 tablespoon chopped fresh rosemary
1 cup white wine
2–3 cups low-sodium chicken stock
1/3 lemon
1 teaspoon lemon zest
1 tablespoon chopped parsley

Season the lamb shanks with the salt and pepper.

Place a roasting pan large enough to hold the shanks in one layer in the oven and heat for 5 minutes. Add the shanks to the pan and brown (no oil is needed, as shanks have enough exterior fat), turning a few times to brown all sides, about 20 minutes. Remove the shanks from the pan and set aside. Pour off all but 2 tablespoons of the rendered fat.

Add the garlic and rosemary to pan, stir, and continue to cook for 2 minutes more, being careful not to burn the garlic. Add the wine and cook to reduce by one-third, about 6 minutes. Return the shanks to the pan and add 2 cups stock to cover no more than one-third the level of the meat. Cover the pan tightly with foil and roast, checking periodically, turning the shanks and adding more stock if necessary, about 3–3 1/2 hours. Remove from oven, squeeze the juice from the lemon over the shanks, add the zest and parsley to the pan juices, and serve.

SERVES 4–6

Lamb Shoulder Braised with Balsamic and Olives

This is another example of a very easy and forgiving braise. The pan searing provides the rich browning, and then the savory liquid infuses flavor throughout the long, slow roast. Don't be intimidated by the anchovies in this recipe, as they melt away and add a saltiness that is one of the *most* important contributors to the tasty result.

LARGE BROWNING FLAME TRANSITIONING TO ROASTING OVEN ENVIRONMENT

6 pounds lamb shoulder
1 tablespoon salt
½ teaspoon freshly ground black pepper
¼ cup olive oil
3 cloves garlic
1 (2-ounce) can anchovies
2 sprigs rosemary, 6 inches each
¼ cup balsamic vinegar
1 cup white wine
4–5 cups low-sodium chicken stock
2 cups whole green olives, such as
    Super Colossal Sicilian Style

Cut lamb shoulder into 4-inch pieces and place in a large bowl. Add the salt and pepper and toss to coat.

Heat a large 3-inch-deep skillet in oven for 3–4 minutes. Remove, add oil, and heat for 30 seconds more. Add lamb to skillet and return to oven. It may be necessary to brown in two batches. (If you overfill and crowd the lamb pieces, they will steam and not brown). Continue to cook until browned on all sides, about 20–30 minutes.

While the lamb is browning, finely chop garlic, anchovies, and rosemary and place in the now empty lamb bowl. Add the vinegar, wine, and 1 cup stock.

Once the lamb is browned, add the anchovy mixture to the pan. Cover tightly and return to the oven. Check periodically to ensure liquid has not evaporated and add more stock when necessary. You want to maintain a liquid level of about one-third of the way up, but not covering, the meat. After 1 hour, add the olives and continue to cook and monitor the liquid for 45 minutes more. Cook until the lamb is fork tender. Remove from oven and serve.

SERVES 6–8

La Porchetta

The most anticipated day of cooking in Tuscany is when we roast La Porchetta! Don't be afraid to roast a whole pig at your next event for this most majestic of presentations. Prepare your senses for slicing into a succulently roasted pig; the aroma from the fresh herbs and the classic Tuscan spice blend is one of the most appetizing that will ever come from your oven.

LARGE BROWNING FLAME TRANSITIONING TO ROASTING OVEN ENVIRONMENT

¼ cup chopped fresh rosemary
¼ cup chopped fresh sage
¼ cup finely chopped garlic
¼ cup salt
Zest from 2 lemons
1 tablespoon freshly ground black pepper
1 (25–30-pound) whole pig
½ cup Tuscan Porchetta Spice (see below)
1 boneless pork loin, about 4–5 pounds
½ cup water

TUSCAN PORCHETTA SPICE
½ cup ground coriander
1 teaspoon ground allspice
1 teaspoon ground cinnamon
1 teaspoon ground nutmeg
1 teaspoon ground cloves
1 teaspoon ground black pepper
1 teaspoon white pepper

Combine the rosemary, sage, garlic, salt, lemon zest, and pepper, and mix well; set aside.

Debone the pig, starting with the rib cage and working all the way down to the hind legs. Be very careful not to puncture the skin. Lay open the pig and rub the herb-salt mixture, followed by the Tuscan Porchetta Spice (directions below), over the entire inside surface. Set the boneless loin into the middle of the pig cavity and wrap the pig skin around the loin. Tie securely at 3-inch intervals with butcher's twine. (This may be completed one day in advance and meat kept in the refrigerator.)

Using aluminum foil, wrap the pig's head, tail, and feet (to prevent burning) and tent the body. Set in a large roasting pan with ½ cup water. Check at 30-minute intervals to baste, record internal temperature, and rotate pan in relation to fire. Total cooking time will be about 3–3½ hours, or until internal temperature is 138°F. Remove and let rest 30 minutes before slicing.

Tuscan Porchetta Spice
Combine all ingredients and use as directed.

SERVES 30–35

Pork Tenderloin Saltimbocca

Enjoy the classic flavors of saltimbocca applied to a pork tenderloin.

LARGE BROWNING FLAME TRANSITIONING TO ROASTING OVEN ENVIRONMENT

PORK

6 cloves garlic, finely chopped

5 tablespoons olive oil, divided

2 teaspoons kosher salt

1/2 teaspoon freshly ground pepper

2 pork tenderloins (about 1 1/2 pounds each)

8 fresh sage leaves

12 slices prosciutto crudo

SAUCE

3 tablespoons extra virgin olive oil

2 tablespoons finely diced shallots

3 cups assorted mushrooms, thinly sliced

1 clove garlic, minced

1 cup dry white wine

2 tablespoons unsalted butter

1 tablespoon finely chopped parsley

3 sage leaves

Freshly ground black pepper and salt, to taste

1/2 lemon

Pinch of freshly grated nutmeg

Combine the garlic, 3 tablespoons oil, salt, and pepper in a small bowl and mix well to a paste-like texture. Rub mixture over the pork tenderloins. Evenly lay sage leaves horizontally over pork.

Place a sheet of plastic on your work surface. Lay 6 prosciutto slices, overlapping their edges, on the plastic. Set one tenderloin onto one far edge of prosciutto and roll, lifting the tenderloin with plastic to enclose with prosciutto and pressing to ensure prosciutto adheres to the meat. When fully wrapped, carefully remove the plastic wrap. Repeat with second tenderloin and set both aside.

Place a large sauté or frying pan in the oven and heat for 5 minutes. Add remaining oil and heat for 30 seconds. Add prosciutto-wrapped tenderloins seam side down and sear for about 2 minutes. Using tongs, roll tenderloins and continue to cook for about 6 minutes, or until lightly browned on all sides. Continue to cook for 15 minutes more, or until internal temperature registers 138°F. Remove tenderloins from pan, cover, and set aside to rest while you make the sauce. Thinly slice the pork tenderloins and serve with the sauce.

Sauce

Return pan to oven with 3 tablespoons oil and heat for 1–2 minutes. Add shallots and cook for 2 minutes. Add mushrooms and cook for 6–8 minutes, or until they've released their liquid and are softened. Add garlic and cook for 1 minute. Add wine, scraping off browned bits from bottom of pan. Add butter, parsley, and sage and cook until butter is melted, about 1 minute. Season with salt, pepper, squeeze of fresh lemon, and nutmeg.

SERVES 6–8

Tuscan Wild Boar Stew

I am fortunate to have a lot of lean, healthy wild game to cook with throughout the year in our cooking classes. Wild boar run through the Mugnaini vineyard and frequently end up in this delicious ragu. It is so much easier to brown the large batches of meat in the wood-burning oven than on a cooktop. You may, of course, substitute with domestic pork; however, if you have the opportunity to use wild boar, you will definitely enjoy its pure, sweet flavors.

LARGE BROWNING FLAME TRANSITIONING TO ROASTING OVEN ENVIRONMENT

2 pounds wild boar, cut into 2-inch pieces

2 small red onions, quartered

2 stalks celery, large dice

3 carrots, large dice

3 sprigs parsley, left whole

1 lemon, cut in half

1 teaspoon salt

½ teaspoon freshly ground pepper

½ cup olive oil

2 cloves garlic, chopped

1 sprig rosemary

1 sprig sage

2 cups meat broth (chicken, veal, or beef), divided

2 cups dry red wine

1 (4-ounce) can tomato paste

3 bay leaves

Combine the meat, onions, celery, carrots, and parsley in a large bowl. Squeeze the lemon over the mixture. Add cold water to cover meat and vegetables completely. Place bowl in refrigerator for 24 hours. Remove bowl from the refrigerator and pour contents into a colander to drain.

Remove the vegetables, rinse with cold water, drain, and set on a cutting board. Chop into small dice (or use a food processor) and set aside. Remove wild boar pieces, rinse with cold water, and drain.

Place a roasting pan in the oven and heat for 5 minutes. Do not add oil yet, as the liquid in the meat will need to evaporate first. Add the wild boar pieces and cook until excess liquid has evaporated. Add salt, pepper, and oil, using tongs to turn meat until well browned. Add the onion, celery, carrots, parsley, garlic, rosemary, and sage and continue to cook until vegetables are lightly browned and softened. Add half the broth and cook for about 30 minutes. Add the wine and heat through. Add the tomato paste, remaining broth, and bay leaves. Cover and cook until meat is fork tender, about 2–2½ hours.

SERVES 4–6

Skewers of Mixed Meat with Pancetta and Sage

These skewered morsels of meat can be enjoyed as an appetizer or entrée. When turned during grilling, they are naturally basted from the pancetta and the oil from the fresh sage leaves. They emerge from the grill lightly charred, juicy, and dripping with flavors.

GRILLING OVEN ENVIRONMENT

MARINADE

½ cup extra virgin olive oil

2 cloves garlic, finely chopped

1 tablespoon freshly chopped rosemary

½ teaspoon salt

¼ teaspoon freshly ground black pepper

MEAT

¼–⅓ pound pork tenderloin or boneless chop, cut into 8 (1-inch) pieces

4 slices pancetta, about ⅛ pound, each slice cut into 4 pieces

16 whole fresh sage leaves

1 large or 2 medium sweet Italian sausage links, about ¼ pound, cut into 8 pieces

¼–⅓ pound boneless lamb (leg or sirloin), cut into 8 (1-inch) pieces

¼–⅓ pound boneless, skinless chicken breast, cut into 8 (1-inch) pieces

8 (10-inch) bamboo skewers, soaked in cold water for 30 minutes

½ lemon

NOTE FROM THE AUTHOR: It is very important to cut meats into the same size pieces for even cooking.

For the marinade, combine all the ingredients in a small bowl and stir to combine; set aside.

Thread the skewers with a piece of pork, followed by a piece of pancetta (fold in half if necessary), a fresh sage leaf, a piece of sausage, and a piece of lamb, followed by another slice of pancetta, a sage leaf, and ending with a piece of chicken. Place skewers on a sheet pan and drizzle with marinade; turn to coat. Cover and refrigerate for 2–3 hours or overnight.

Heat grill for 5 minutes. Cook for 6–8 minutes, turning every 1–2 minutes, or until browned and cooked through. Remove and then squeeze lemon over top. Let rest for 5 minutes before serving.

SERVES 4

Roasted Pork Loin with Fig Sauce

For easy entertaining, the sauce for this recipe can be prepared the day before. The pork can also be seasoned a day in advance, and both can be kept in the refrigerator. Because it is boneless, this large roast has a fairly short cooking time and feeds a large crowd.

LARGE BROWNING FLAME TRANSITIONING TO ROASTING OVEN ENVIRONMENT

FIG SAUCE

3 cups port
1 cup low-sodium chicken broth
10 dried black mission figs, coarsely chopped
2 sprigs fresh rosemary
1 sprig fresh thyme
1 cinnamon stick
3 whole allspice
1/2 teaspoon dried fennel seeds
1 tablespoon honey
2 tablespoons unsalted butter, cut into pieces
1/4 teaspoon salt
1/4 teaspoon freshly ground black pepper

PORK

2 tablespoons olive oil
2 tablespoons finely chopped fresh rosemary
1 tablespoon finely chopped fresh thyme
1 tablespoon salt
1 teaspoon freshly ground black pepper
1 (4 1/2–5-pound) boneless pork loin

To make the Fig Sauce, combine the port, broth, figs, rosemary, thyme, cinnamon stick, allspice, fennel seeds, and honey in a saucepan. Boil over medium-high heat until reduced by half, about 30 minutes. Discard the rosemary and thyme sprigs and the cinnamon stick. Pour contents of the pan into a blender and puree until smooth. Blend in the butter, salt, and pepper. (The sauce can be made 1 day ahead. Cover and refrigerate. Rewarm over medium heat before using.)

To make the pork, put the oil, rosemary, thyme, salt, and pepper in a small bowl and stir to combine. Spread the herb mixture over the pork to coat completely. Place a heavy-bottom roasting pan in the oven and heat for 5 minutes. Add the pork loin and brown evenly, turning with tongs. Continue to roast until an internal thermometer inserted into the center of the pork registers 138°F, about 45 minutes. Transfer the pork to a cutting board and tent with foil to keep warm. Let the pork rest for 15 minutes.

To serve, slice diagonally into 1/4-inch slices and serve drizzled with warm Fig Sauce.

SERVES 8–10

Roasted Fillet of Beef Stuffed with Prosciutto and Parmigiano

This is our deliciously dressed-up version of the basic roasted tenderloin. Perfect for elegant dining or holiday entertaining.

LARGE BROWNING FLAME TRANSITIONING TO ROASTING OVEN ENVIRONMENT

1 (3½-pound) whole beef tenderloin, trimmed
3 teaspoons salt, divided
1½ teaspoons freshly ground pepper, divided
1 teaspoon finely chopped fresh rosemary
3 teaspoons finely chopped parsley
1 clove garlic, finely chopped
8 thin slices prosciutto crudo
¼ cup freshly grated Parmigiano-Reggiano
4 tablespoons extra virgin olive oil, divided
Butcher's twine

Butterfly the tenderloin, place between two pieces of plastic, and pound until thin and even in thickness, about ½ inch. With the cut side up, season with 2 teaspoons salt and 1 teaspoon pepper, and rub with the rosemary, parsley, and garlic. Cover tenderloin with the prosciutto slices, overlapping edges, and sprinkle with the Parmigiano-Reggiano. Drizzle with 2 tablespoons oil.

Starting with the long end and using the plastic underneath, roll tightly and tie with butcher's twine at 2-inch intervals. Season the outside of the beef with the remaining salt and pepper. (The roast can be prepared up to this point several hours ahead, covered tightly with plastic, and refrigerated. Bring to room temperature before cooking.) Place a half sheet pan in the oven and allow to heat for 5 minutes. Add the remaining oil and heat for another 30 seconds. Place the tenderloin seam side down on the hot sheet pan and return to the oven.

Using tongs, roll the tenderloin and brown evenly. Continue to roast for about 25–30 minutes, checking the internal temperature every 5 minutes until internal temperature of the middle section of the tenderloin reaches 120°F. This will allow for a range of doneness, rare in the mid-section progressing to well done on the ends. Remove from oven, cover, and allow to rest for 10 minutes before carving.

SERVES 6–8

VEGETABLES

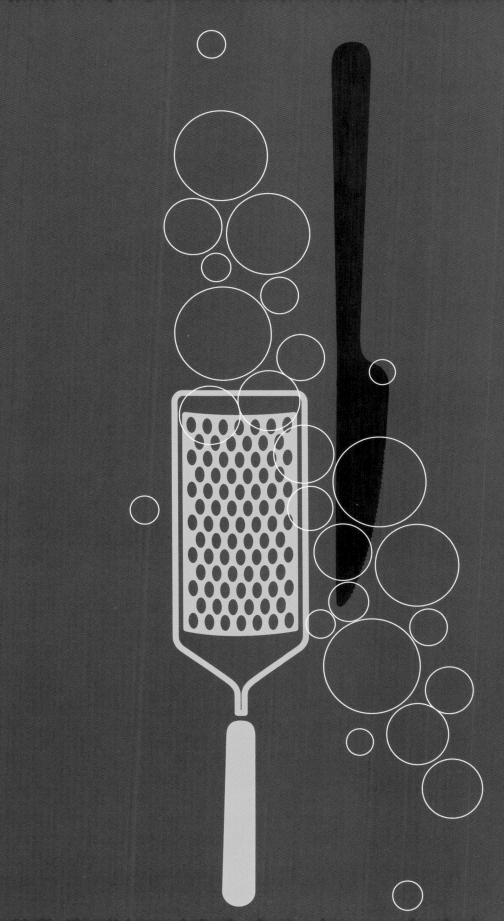

Wood-Roasted Eggplant Parmigiano

Roasting the eggplant instead of frying it produces a light, fresh version of this classic dish. It is, of course, a summertime favorite! If you have any leftover roasted peppers, add a layer along with the other ingredients for a change.

ROASTING OVEN ENVIRONMENT

Oil
3 large eggplants
2 teaspoons kosher salt
2 tablespoons extra virgin olive oil
2 cloves garlic
4 cups canned whole San Marzano tomatoes, with juice
Pinch of cinnamon
½ cup fresh basil leaves, torn into 2–3 pieces
1 pound fresh mozzarella, thinly sliced
½ cup freshly grated Parmigiano-Reggiano cheese

Peel the eggplants and then slice into ½-inch rounds; set on an oiled sheet pan. Place in wood-burning oven and roast under large flame (best to prep in perimeter burn during startup) for 2 minutes, or until tops are lightly browned. Turn the eggplant slices over and repeat with other side. When lightly browned on both sides and slightly tender, remove from oven and sprinkle with salt; set aside.

Place a large sauté pan with olive oil in the oven and heat. Add garlic and cook for 1 minute. Add tomatoes and cinnamon and cook for 20–30 minutes, or until tomatoes break easily with the back of a spoon; remove and set aside. (Sauce may be prepared two days in advance and stored in refrigerator.)

To assemble, oil the inside of a ceramic baking dish and line bottom with slices of eggplant. Cover with the tomato sauce, top with one-third of the basil leaves and one-third of the mozzarella, and sprinkle with one-third of the Parmigiano-Reggiano. Repeat two more layers with remaining ingredients. Drizzle top of completed dish with oil and bake in oven for 20–30 minutes, or until heated through and bubbling slightly. (Do not overcook or allow to boil or cheese will be rubbery.) Remove and let rest for 10 minutes before serving.

SERVES 6–8

Roasted Asparagus with Lemon and Parmigiano Shavings

Cut the woody section from the asparagus stems, and then place stems in a container with 1 inch of water and refrigerate until ready to use. This will ensure the vegetables' crispness and turgor, which will allow them to cook more quickly.

ROASTING OVEN ENVIRONMENT

2 pounds asparagus
1 tablespoon extra virgin olive oil
1/2 lemon
1/8 teaspoon salt
Freshly ground black pepper
Parmigiano-Reggiano shavings

Rinse the asparagus and remove any remaining woody section from stem end with a diagonal cut.

Peel 2- to 3-inch lengths of the exterior green skin from end of stalks. Place prepared asparagus on a sheet pan or large sauté pan in a single layer. Drizzle with oil and toss to coat. Set in wood-burning oven and cook 4–5 minutes, shaking pan a few times to turn asparagus. Remove and squeeze lemon over asparagus. Add the salt and pepper and sprinkle with Parmigiano-Reggiano shavings.

SERVES 4

Roasted Potatoes with Rosemary and Garlic

This is a year-round favorite. These potatoes are almost always eaten off the roasting pan and never make it to the table.

ROASTING OVEN ENVIRONMENT

2 pounds Yukon gold potatoes, unpeeled and
    cut into 2-inch pieces
1/4 cup extra virgin olive oil
4 cloves garlic, whole and unpeeled
3 sprigs fresh rosemary, about 4 inches each
2 teaspoons kosher salt and freshly ground pepper

Place the potatoes on a sheet pan and toss with oil to coat. Press the garlic cloves and rosemary onto the pan with the potatoes.

Set pan in oven and roast uncovered (do not stir potatoes during roasting) for about 20–25 minutes, or until tender. (If you have too much flame or top heat, loosely cover the pan with foil for part of the roasting time).

Remove from oven, season with salt and pepper, and let rest for 10 minutes (this will ensure that potatoes will not stick to the pan).

SERVES 4

Zucchini Gratin with Tomatoes and Gruyère

This works well as a stand-alone dish for lunch or served as an accompaniment with roasted chicken. Of course, it's always best prepared during summer months.

ROASTING OVEN ENVIRONMENT

2 pounds fresh zucchini (about 3–4 medium zucchini)

½ small red onion

6 medium fresh plum tomatoes

3 tablespoons extra virgin olive oil

1 teaspoon kosher salt

1 teaspoon herbes de Provence (or chopped thyme, marjoram, or savory)

1 teaspoon freshly ground black pepper

1 cup grated Gruyère cheese

Olive oil

Rinse the zucchini and cut and discard ends; thinly slice into ⅛-inch rounds. Cut onion in half and thinly slice. Slice tomatoes lengthwise into ¼-inch slices. Place the zucchini, onion, oil, salt, herbes de Provence, pepper, and cheese in a large mixing bowl; mix well.

Oil the inside of a ceramic baking dish and add zucchini mixture. Lay the tomato slices overlapping to cover the zucchini. Drizzle with oil and set in the oven. Bake for about 40 minutes, or until vegetables are tender, the top is bubbling lightly, and tomatoes are lightly charred. Remove and let rest for 10 minutes before serving.

SERVES 4

Roasted Cauliflower with Garlic Anchovy Sauce and Pecorino

If you have never tasted cauliflower crisped at a high temperature, you are missing a real treat. Don't be intimidated by the anchovy sauce and pecorino, as they melt into the recipe and add the salt and seasoning for this uniquely flavored dish.

PIZZA OVEN OR ROASTING OVEN ENVIRONMENT

¼ cup plus 2 tablespoons extra virgin
    olive oil, divided
3 whole anchovies in oil, drained
1 clove garlic
Pinch of red pepper flakes
1 large (2-pound) fresh head cauliflower
¼ cup grated pecorino cheese
1 tablespoon chopped parsley

Place a small sauté pan in the mouth of the oven with ¼ cup oil and the anchovies. Heat for about 2 minutes to dissolve anchovies, stirring as needed. Do not burn. Smash garlic clove with the tip of a knife, finely chop, and add to sauté pan along with red pepper flakes. Cook for about 1 minute; remove and set aside.

Rinse cauliflower and remove the green leaves at the base. (Do not remove the solid core). Set cauliflower upright on a cutting board and slice in half lengthwise. Slice each half into ¼-inch slices. Set sliced cauliflower on a sheet pan, drizzle with remaining oil, and toss well to coat. Set in the oven and roast for 10 minutes. Remove and add anchovy sauce and pecorino, mixing well. Return to oven for 3–5 minutes more, or until tender with browned crisp edges. Remove, sprinkle with parsley, and serve.

SERVES 4

Yukon Gold Potato Gratin with Gruyère and Fresh Thyme

Everyone loves the rich combination of baked potatoes and cheese!

BAKE OVEN ENVIRONMENT

2 cups half-and-half
1 clove garlic
1 sprig fresh thyme, about 2 inches long
2 pounds Yukon gold potatoes
Oil
Kosher salt and freshly ground black pepper
3 cups grated Gruyère cheese, 1/2 cup reserved
Freshly grated nutmeg

Place half-and-half, garlic, and thyme in a sauce-pan; bring to a simmer and keep warm. Before using, remove garlic clove and thyme stem.

Peel the potatoes and thinly slice. Oil a ceramic baking dish. Arrange potato slices on bottom of dish, overlapping edges. Season potatoes with salt and pepper; cover with one-third of the heated half-and-half and top with one-third of the cheese and a sprinkle of nutmeg. Repeat with two more layers. Top gratin with reserved cheese. Bake in a wood-burning oven for 40–45 minutes, or until potatoes are tender when pierced with the tip of a knife and the top is golden brown. If top is over-browning, cover very loosely with foil. Remove and let rest for 15 minutes before cutting to serve.

SERVES 6

Roasted Fennel, Carrots, and Cipollini

This is a good fall and winter accompaniment to roasted meats.

ROASTING OVEN ENVIRONMENT

2 fennel bulbs (fronds reserved)

8 medium carrots

2 cups cipollini onions

2 tablespoons extra virgin olive oil

2 teaspoons kosher salt

1 tablespoon finely chopped parsley

2 teaspoons chopped reserved fennel fronds

Rinse the fennel bulbs and remove stems and fronds, reserving fronds. Quarter the bulbs lengthwise and remove tough center core. Slice quarters into 2–3 wedges each. Rinse and peel carrots, slice lengthwise, and then cut diagonally into 2-inch pieces. Peel skins from cipollini.

Place all vegetables onto a sheet pan, drizzle with the oil, and toss to coat. Set pan in the oven and roast vegetables, stirring occasionally, for about 30 minutes, or until they are softened and lightly browned. Remove from oven and then add salt, parsley, and fennel fronds. Toss well to combine and serve.

SERVES 6–8

Overnight Cannellini Beans Tuscan Style

This recipe is a perfect example of the benefits of cooking with retained heat. The slow overnight cooking produces tender beans with a very thick, creamy broth not possible to achieve on a cooktop. Use our terra-cotta bean pot for the best results and presentation!

OVERNIGHT LOW TEMPERATURE ENVIRONMENT

2 cups dry cannellini beans
8 cups cold water
1 tablespoon extra virgin olive oil
2 sprigs fresh sage
6 whole black peppercorns
Salt, to taste

Soak beans in cold water for 6–8 hours. Drain, rinse, and place in a terra-cotta bean pot. Add 8 cups cold water, oil, sage, and peppercorns. Cover and set in low-temperature oven (about 350ºF) overnight. Remove from oven and season with salt.

SERVES 6

Sweet Stuffed Peppers

This recipe can be used as an appetizer or first plate.

PIZZA OVEN OR ROASTING OVEN ENVIRONMENT

3 red or yellow sweet peppers, roasted
   (to roast, see page 68)
1/3 pound smoked mozzarella cheese
2 tablespoons capers, chopped
12 fresh basil leaves
2 tablespoons grated Parmigiano-Reggiano
   cheese
Olive oil

Slice each roasted pepper into halves lengthwise and lay out on work surface with the insides facing up. Cut the mozzarella cheese into 6 rectangular pieces. Place a few capers and 2 basil leaves on each pepper. Top with a slice of cheese. Roll peppers as tightly as possible and place seam side down in an oiled ceramic baker. Sprinkle with Parmigiano-Reggiano and drizzle with oil. Set in oven and bake until heated through, about 10 minutes.

SERVES 6

Oven-Roasted Honey-Glazed Root Vegetables

This dish is ideal for fall and winter. Roasting concentrates the sweet flavors of these root vegetables so they can be served plain as well.

ROASTING OVEN ENVIRONMENT

1 pound parsnips
1 pound carrots
1 celery root
1 pound small golden beets
1/3 cup extra virgin olive oil
2 teaspoons chopped fresh thyme
1 teaspoon kosher salt
2 tablespoons water
1 tablespoon honey
Drizzle of balsamic vinegar

Peel the parsnips and carrots and slice diagonally into 1/2-inch pieces. Peel the celery root, cut into quarters, and then cut into 1/2-inch slices. Peel beets and leave whole.

Combine the parsnips, carrots, celery root, and beets in a roasting pan and toss with the oil, thyme, and salt. Add water to the pan and cover with foil. Set in the oven and roast for 45 minutes, or until tender when pierced with the tip of a knife.

Blend honey and vinegar together. Remove vegetables from oven, uncover, and add honey mixture. Stir well and cook for another 10 minutes to thicken pan juices.

SERVES 6–8

Brussels Sprouts with Roasted Garlic and Pancetta

Brussels sprouts are yet another vegetable transformed by the wood-fired oven. Our cooking school converts non-believers into Brussels sprouts lovers every time we feature this recipe in a class.

ROASTING OVEN ENVIRONMENT

20 Brussels sprouts
1 tablespoon extra virgin olive oil
1/2 cup finely diced pancetta
3 cloves roasted garlic, coarsely chopped*
Freshly ground black pepper and salt, to taste

Prepare a pot of boiling salted water and a bowl of ice water. Rinse the Brussels sprouts, remove any yellow outer leaves, and trim stem. Place Brussels sprouts in boiling water and cook for 3 minutes (or 4 minutes for large Brussels sprouts). Remove, drain, and set in ice water; once cool, drain again.

Slice Brussels sprouts in half and place on a sheet pan. Drizzle with oil and then add the pancetta and garlic; toss well to coat. Set in the wood-burning oven and roast for about 10 minutes, or until tender and lightly browned. Remove; add salt and pepper to taste.

*To roast the garlic, cut the top from a whole head of garlic (or more if you wish). Set in a small terra-cotta dish, drizzle with olive oil, add 1 tablespoon water, and cover. Set in the oven and roast for about 20 minutes, or until light caramel in color and soft (or, alternately, do the same with foil instead of a dish).

SERVES 4

Roasted Tomato Bruschetta

We also enjoy these tomatoes tossed with pasta and a little Parmigiano-Reggiano cheese.

PIZZA OVEN OR ROASTING OVEN ENVIRONMENT

2 baskets small cherry tomatoes
2 tablespoons extra virgin olive oil
2 cloves garlic, thinly sliced
1/2 teaspoon kosher salt
4 large basil leaves, chiffonade
6 slices rustic Italian bread, halved

Rinse the tomatoes and place on a sheet pan with the oil and garlic. Toss to coat and set in the oven. Cook until slightly charred and softened. Remove from oven; add salt and basil.

Set bread slices on a sheet pan and place in the wood-burning oven. Cook for 1–2 minutes, or until lightly browned on top. Remove and top with roasted tomatoes and all the pan juices.

SERVES 12

Ratatouille

The bounty of the garden is captured in this dish. Enjoy large batches warm or at room temperature.

ROASTING OVEN ENVIRONMENT

2 large eggplants

8 small zucchini

4 bell peppers (mixed red/yellow/green),
  roasted and peeled (to roast, see page 68)

3 cloves garlic

1/2 cup extra virgin olive oil, plus more as needed

2 sprigs fresh thyme, 3 inches long

3 cups canned whole San Marzano tomatoes,
  with juices

2 teaspoons kosher salt

Freshly ground black pepper

1/2 cup fresh basil leaves

Peel the eggplants if skins are tough; otherwise leave unpeeled. Cut eggplants in half lengthwise and then quarter. Cut quartered sections into 2-inch-long pieces. Prepare the zucchini in the same manner. Cut the peppers into strips about 2–3 inches long. Cut the garlic cloves in half.

Place a saucepan large enough to hold all of the ingredients in oven with the oil, garlic, and thyme. Heat and once browned, remove garlic and the thyme stems; add eggplant. Cook for 8–10 minutes, or until eggplant is lightly browned. Remove eggplant from pan and set aside in a bowl.

Add zucchini to saucepan with additional oil as necessary, return to oven, and cook 6–8 minutes, or until lightly browned. Pull saucepan forward in oven, add eggplant to zucchini along with any accumulated juices in the bowl. Add peppers, tomatoes, salt, pepper, and basil; stir to combine. Cover and set back in the oven to cook for 20–30 minutes more.

SERVES 6–8

Wood-Roasted Corn-on-the-Cob

We enjoy this quick roasted corn-on-the-cob fresh from the garden. Cut corn from the cob to enhance relishes, salsas, and salads.

PIZZA OVEN OR ROASTING OVEN ENVIRONMENT

4 ears fresh corn
1 tablespoon extra virgin olive oil
Salt, to taste

Completely remove the husks and silk from corn. Set cobs on a roasting pan and drizzle with oil to coat. Place in a wood-burning oven and roast for about 6–8 minutes, shaking pan to roll ears for even charring. Do not over-char or corn will lose its sweet fresh taste. Season with salt to taste.

SERVES 4

Braised Shallots

Use this tangy accompaniment as a side with roasted meats and poultry.

ROASTING OVEN ENVIRONMENT

1½ pounds medium shallots (or cipollini or pearl onions)
3 whole cloves
2 tablespoons extra virgin olive oil
1 cup broth (chicken, veal, or beef)
2 teaspoons sugar
1 tablespoon balsamic vinegar
Salt and pepper, to taste
1 teaspoon chopped parsley

Remove skins from shallots and leave whole. Place shallots in a sauté pan with cloves and oil; toss to coat. Set uncovered in the wood-burning oven and cook, stirring a few times, for about 5–6 minutes, or until lightly browned. Add broth, cover, and cook until slightly tender, about 10–15 minutes. Uncover; add sugar and vinegar. Stir and cook for 5–10 minutes more to thicken juices. Remove, season with salt and pepper, add parsley, and serve.

SERVES 4

Twice-Cooked Vegetable Soup

This Tuscan classic is enjoyed warm the day it's made or days later served at room temperature drizzled with good-quality olive oil. Plan ahead and cook your beans overnight in the oven for an authentic flavor.

BAKE OVEN ENVIRONMENT

½ cup olive oil, plus more for drizzling

4 carrots, coarsely chopped

2 stalks celery, coarsely chopped (leaves removed and reserved)

2 red onions, coarsely chopped

3 Yukon gold potatoes, coarsely chopped

3 zucchini, coarsely chopped

1 bunch kale, center stem removed and leaves coarsely chopped

½ head savoy cabbage, coarsely chopped

Sofrito (see below)

3 cups water, plus more if needed

3 cups cooked cannellini beans with 2 cups of their cooking liquid (see Overnight Cannellini Beans, page 130)

½ pound rustic bread, sliced ½ inch thick

½ cup grated Parmigiano-Reggiano cheese

SOFRITO

2 tablespoons olive oil

1 cup canned San Marzano or other good-quality tomatoes, undrained and left whole

2 cloves garlic

2 sprigs fresh rosemary, about 3 inches, leaves removed and stems discarded

½ cup celery leaves (reserved from above)

Place a large stockpot with the oil in the oven and heat. Add the carrots, celery, and onions and cook, stirring a few times, for about 10 minutes, or until vegetables start to soften. Add the potatoes, zucchini, kale, and cabbage and cook for 10 minutes more, stirring occasionally, while you make the sofrito (directions below).

Remove the vegetables from the oven and add the water, beans with their cooking liquid, and the Sofrito. Additional water may be needed to cover vegetables. Cover and set back in the oven to cook for 30 minutes.

To assemble, place bread slices on a sheet pan and set in the oven. Cook until lightly brown on top side only; remove. Place bread slices to partially cover bottom of a terra-cotta casserole dish and ladle soup over bread. Sprinkle with Parmigiano-Reggiano and repeat layers of bread, soup, and cheese to fill dish. Place in the oven and bake for 20 minutes, or until heated through and lightly toasted on top. Remove and stir to mix well. Spoon into serving bowls and drizzle with oil. Soup may be made a day in advance, refrigerated and assembled later.

Sofrito

Place a small sauté pan with the olive oil, tomatoes, garlic, rosemary, and celery leaves in the oven and cook for 10 minutes. Remove, let cool slightly, and place in a food processor and puree.

SERVES 6–8

Roasted Butternut Squash Soup

Roasting the butternut squash intensifies its flavor before it is combined with the remainder of the ingredients to produce this delicious soup.

ROASTING OVEN ENVIRONMENT

5 pounds butternut squash, peeled and cut into
    1-inch pieces
1 yellow onion, cut into 1-inch pieces
3 large carrots, peeled and cut into
    1/2-inch rounds
3 tablespoons olive oil
1 teaspoon kosher salt
6–7 cups low-sodium chicken or vegetable stock
1/2 teaspoon freshly ground black pepper

GARNISH

1 (8-ounce) container Greek yogurt
1 tablespoon lime juice
1 teaspoon lime zest
1/4 teaspoon salt

Place the vegetables in a large bowl, add the oil and salt, and toss to coat. Divide the mixture between two half sheet pans and place in the oven. Roast for about 20 minutes, or until the mixture is nicely browned. It does not have to be fully cooked through. Place vegetables in a large stockpot, add the stock, and cover. Return to the oven and cook until very soft, about 45 minutes.

Remove from heat and puree with an immersion blender, or puree in batches in a blender. For an even smoother soup, pass through a fine-mesh strainer. Add the pepper and taste for seasoning. If a thinner soup is desired, add more stock and heat through.

Mix all of the garnish ingredients together in a small bowl. To serve, ladle soup into bowls and add a teaspoon of garnish mixture on top.

SERVES 4

Mushroom Fricassee

A classic accompaniment to roasted meats and poultry.

PIZZA OVEN OR ROASTING OVEN ENVIRONMENT

1½ pounds assorted mushrooms (cremini,
   shiitake, trumpet royale, etc.)
1 clove garlic
2 small shallots
3 tablespoons extra virgin olive oil
1 tablespoon chopped fresh parsley
1 teaspoon chopped fresh tarragon
¼ cup dry white wine
½ cup chicken stock
¼ cup cream
Pinch of freshly grated nutmeg
Salt and freshly ground black pepper

Clean mushrooms well. Thinly slice the large and medium-size mushrooms and leave the small mushrooms whole. Finely dice the garlic and shallot.

Set a large frying or sauté pan in the oven with the oil and heat. Add mushrooms and cook for about 10 minutes, or until most of the released liquid has evaporated. Add the garlic, shallots, and herbs and cook for about 3 minutes. Add wine and cook for about 2 minutes, or until it evaporates. Add stock, cream, and nutmeg; cook for a few minutes to thicken. Remove and season with salt and pepper.

SERVES 4

PASTA, RICE, AND EGGS

Lasagna with Tomato Sauce and Sheep's Milk Ricotta

In our Healdsburg Cooking School, we are lucky to have access to artisan cheese products of the local Bellwether Farms. One of these is their farm fresh sheep's milk ricotta. Never mushy or grainy, its sweet creaminess makes this simply flavored lasagna light and delicate. The sauce can be cooked while the oven is in pizza oven environment, and then the lasagna can be baked once the oven temperature drops to the roasting oven environment.

PIZZA OVEN ENVIRONMENT AND ROASTING OVEN ENVIRONMENT

1 pound fresh sheep's milk ricotta

8 ounces fresh mozzarella, diced

1/2 cup freshly grated Parmigiano-Reggiano cheese, divided

2 tablespoons unsalted butter

1/2 teaspoon kosher salt

Freshly grated black pepper

Freshly grated nutmeg

Tomato Sauce (see below)

1 pound fresh lasagna, boiled al dente, drained and set aside

1 cup fresh basil leaves, torn

TOMATO SAUCE

1/4 cup extra virgin olive oil

2 cloves garlic, thinly sliced

2 (14-ounce) cans San Marzano or other good-quality tomatoes, drained and left whole

2 teaspoons kosher salt

Pinch of cinnamon

Combine the ricotta, mozzarella, 1/4 cup Parmigiano-Reggiano, butter, salt, pepper, and nutmeg in a mixing bowl and stir lightly to combine. Prepare the Tomato Sauce (directions below).

To assemble, oil a rectangle 9 x 12-inch ceramic baking dish. Line bottom of baking dish with pasta sheets and top with one-third of the Tomato Sauce and half of the basil. Top with another layer of pasta and cover with half of the cheese mixture. Top cheese with another layer of pasta and repeat with another layer each of sauce with basil and cheese mixture. Finish top layer of pasta with sauce and sprinkle with remaining Parmigiano-Reggiano. Bake for about 30 minutes, or until heated through and bubbling.

Tomato Sauce

Place a large sauté pan with oil in the oven and heat. Add garlic and cook for 1–2 minutes, or until fragrant. Add the tomatoes, salt, and cinnamon. Cook for 20 minutes, or until tomatoes break easily with the back of a spoon and the sauce has slightly thickened.

SERVES 10–12

Risotto with Summer Tomato

Once you make a risotto in the wood-burning oven, you will never go back to the cooktop. With the high overhead heat of the oven, you do not have to stir continuously and the risotto comes together faster.

ROASTING OVEN ENVIRONMENT

2 pounds heirloom tomatoes
5 cups chicken stock
2 tablespoons extra virgin olive oil
½ cup finely chopped shallots
2 cups Arborio rice
2 tablespoons unsalted butter
½ cup freshly grated Parmigiano-Reggiano, plus more for serving
Freshly ground black pepper

Using a tomato peeler or vegetable peeler, remove skins from the tomatoes and cut each tomato in half. Set a fine sieve over a bowl and squeeze the tomato halves into the sieve. Discard the seeds, reserve the juice, and finely chop the tomato flesh; set juice and chopped tomatoes aside.

Combine the stock and reserved tomato juice in a saucepan and heat.

Set a heavy-bottom sauté pan in the foreground of the wood-burning oven with the oil and shallots. Sauté, stirring frequently, until light golden and soft, about 3–5 minutes. Do not allow to burn.

Add rice and stir to coat with oil and heat through, about 3 minutes. Add hot stock mixture to cover rice, about 1 cup. Stir a few times and then let sit in oven without stirring until liquid is absorbed. Add more stock and repeat, stirring occasionally and letting each batch of additional stock absorb before adding the next. Total cooking time should be about 20 minutes for rice to be al dente. Remove from oven at that point and stir vigorously to increase creaminess. Add butter, Parmigiano-Reggiano, and diced tomato and stir to combine. Serve with a sprinkle of additional Parmigiano-Reggiano and a twist of freshly ground black pepper.

SERVES 6

Risotto with Roasted Butternut Squash and Prosciutto

3/4 pound butternut squash, peeled

1/4 cup finely diced prosciutto

1 teaspoon chopped fresh thyme

3 tablespoons extra virgin olive oil, divided

1/2 cup finely chopped shallots

2 cups Arborio rice

6 cups chicken stock, heated

1 tablespoon unsalted butter

1/2 cup freshly grated Parmigiano-Reggiano cheese

Dice the squash into 1-inch cubes and place in a sheet pan along with the prosciutto and thyme. Drizzle with 1 tablespoon oil. Toss well to coat and spread out in a single layer. Set in the wood-burning oven and roast until squash is slightly tender, about 6–8 minutes. Do not fully cook the squash at this point, as it will complete cooking in the risotto. Remove from oven and set aside.

Set a heavy-bottom sauté pan in the foreground of the oven with shallots and remaining oil. Sauté until softened, about 3–5 minutes. Do not burn.

Add the rice to the pan, stir to coat with the oil, and cook for about 3 minutes, or until lightly toasted and well heated. Add stock to just cover rice, about 1 cup; stir, and then let sit in oven without stirring until liquid has been absorbed, about 5 minutes. Repeat, stirring occasionally and allowing each addition of stock to absorb before adding the next. After 15 minutes, add the squash mixture and stir well to combine. Continue to cook risotto for another 5 minutes, or until rice is al dente. Remove from oven and stir vigorously to increase creaminess. Stir in butter and cheese and serve.

SERVES 6

Risotto with Seafood

5 tablespoons extra virgin olive oil, divided

2 cloves garlic, lightly crushed

Pinch of dry red chile flakes

Peel from 1/2 lemon

1 bay leaf

1 sprig fresh thyme, about 2 inches long

1/2 cup dry white wine

2 dozen small clams

1 pound shrimp, shells removed and deveined

1/2 pound calamari, cut into 1/4-inch rings

2 tablespoons extra virgin olive oil

1/4 cup finely chopped shallots

2 cups Arborio rice

6 cups seafood stock, heated

1 tablespoon chopped parsley

Set a large sauté pan in the wood-burning oven with 3 tablespoons oil, garlic, red chile, lemon peel, bay leaf, and thyme. Cook for about 5 minutes to infuse oil. Remove garlic when golden brown. Add wine and clams. Cover and cook for about 3 minutes, or until clams open slightly. Remove pan from oven, add shrimp and calamari, cover, and set aside.

Set a large heavy-bottom sauté pan in the foreground of the wood-burning oven with remaining oil and shallots. Cook for about 3–5 minutes, stirring a few times until shallots are softened. Do not burn. Add the rice and stir well to coat with oil; cook for 3 minutes to heat well. Add stock to cover rice, about 1 cup; stir, and leave in oven for about 5 minutes, or until liquid has been absorbed. Repeat with remaining stock until rice is cooked through but remains firm and al dente.

Remove from oven, add contents of seafood pan and the parsley, and stir to combine. Serve immediately.

SERVES 6

Risotto with Asparagus, Fresh Peas, and Lemon

ROASTING OVEN ENVIRONMENT

1 bunch asparagus

2 cups freshly shelled green peas

¼ cup extra virgin olive oil, divided

1 clove garlic, minced

Salt, to taste

1 tablespoon chopped fresh parsley

3 tablespoons unsalted butter, divided

¼ cup finely chopped shallots

2 cups Arborio rice

6–7 cups chicken or vegetable stock, heated

½ cup freshly grated Asiago cheese

Freshly ground black pepper

Rinse the asparagus and remove the tough stem ends. Cut on the diagonal into 1-inch pieces. Rinse peas and set aside. Set a small sauté pan in the wood-burning oven with half of the oil and the garlic. Heat and add asparagus and peas. Cook for about 5 minutes, remove from oven, season with salt, and stir in parsley; set aside.

Set a heavy-bottom sauté pan in the foreground of the wood-burning oven with the remaining oil, 1 tablespoon butter, and shallots. Sauté, stirring frequently, until softened, about 3–5 minutes.

Add rice and stir to coat in oil and butter. Cook for about 5 minutes, or until lightly toasted and heated through. Add enough stock to cover rice, about 1 cup; stir and let sit in oven without stirring until liquid has been absorbed. Continue to add stock at intervals, stirring and allowing liquid to absorb before adding more stock.

After 15 minutes cooking time, add the asparagus and pea mixture along with more stock, and cook for 5 minutes longer, or until rice is al dente. Remove from oven and stir vigorously to increase creaminess. Add remaining butter and cheese and mix well. Serve with freshly ground black pepper.

6 SERVINGS

Baked Rigatoni Puttanesca

Baking pasta is a nice way to transform your leftover ingredients from a pizza party into a satisfying meal.

ROASTING OVEN ENVIRONMENT OR BAKE OVEN ENVIRONMENT

1 pound rigatoni, cooked al dente in boiling salted water, drained well, rinsed, and set aside in a large mixing bowl

¼ cup extra virgin olive oil

3 cloves garlic, finely chopped

1 (2–ounce) can anchovy fillets in oil, drained and coarsely chopped

2 small dried red chiles, chopped

2 tablespoons capers in salt, soaked, drained, and rinsed well

½ cup coarsely chopped kalamata olives

2 (14-ounce) cans whole San Marzano or other good-quality tomatoes, with juice

2 tablespoons chopped fresh parsley

8 ounces fresh mozzarella cheese, diced

¼ cup freshly grated Parmigiano-Reggiano cheese

Prepare the pasta.

Set a large sauté pan in the oven with the oil, garlic, anchovies, red chiles, capers, and olives and cook for about 3–5 minutes to fully infuse oil with all the flavors. Add the tomatoes, stir, and continue cooking for about 15 minutes, or until the tomatoes break easily with the back of a spoon. Remove and stir in parsley.

Pour sauce over rigatoni, add mozzarella, and toss well. Pour into an oiled ceramic baking dish, sprinkle with Parmigiano, and place in the oven. Bake for about 15 minutes, or until heated through and golden brown on top.

SERVES 6

Oven-Roasted Vegetable and Pancetta Strata

Served warm from the oven, this works equally well for brunch or lunch when served with a green salad. All the prep can be done during the perimeter burn or while waiting for the oven to drop to a bake environment, which makes assembly easy.

BAKE OVEN ENVIRONMENT

1-pound loaf French bread, cut into
    1-inch-thick slices
2 tablespoons olive oil, divided
8 ounces pancetta, cut into half rounds
    and then 1/2-inch dice
1 pound button mushrooms, cut into
    1/2-inch slices
1 teaspoon chopped fresh thyme
5 ounces baby spinach
2 tablespoons unsalted butter
2 red bell peppers, roasted and cut into large
    dice (to roast, see page 68)
2 cups grated Gruyère cheese
2 cups half-and-half
10 eggs
1 teaspoon salt
1/2 teaspoon pepper
1/2 teaspoon smoked paprika
1/4 teaspoon dry mustard
1/2 teaspoon dried oregano
1/4 teaspoon dried chile flakes
1/4 cup grated Parmigiano-Reggiano cheese

Place the sliced bread on a sheet pan, put in the oven, and lightly toast for about 3 minutes, turning halfway through cooking time; set aside to cool.

In a sauté pan, add 1 tablespoon oil and pancetta; place in the oven, stirring occasionally, for about 8 minutes, or until fat has rendered and the pancetta has browned. Remove from pan and set aside.

Pour off all but about 1 tablespoon of the fat and add the mushrooms and thyme. Cook for about 8 minutes, stirring occasionally, until the mushrooms have softened and the juices have evaporated. Remove from pan and set aside to cool.

Place the spinach on a quarter sheet pan and drizzle with remaining oil. Place in oven and cook until just wilted, about 2 minutes.

Butter one side of the bread and place buttered side down in a 9 x 12-inch ceramic baking dish. Top with the mushrooms, bell peppers, spinach, and Gruyère.

In a large bowl, whisk the half-and-half, eggs, and all remaining herbs and spices together. Gently pour over the layered mixture. Top with the Parmigiano-Reggiano. Allow mixture to rest at room temperature for 1 hour, gently pressing bread down occasionally to submerge and thoroughly saturate. Place in the oven, close door, and bake for 18–20 minutes. Let stand for 10–15 minutes before cutting and serving.

SERVES 8–10

Oven-Poached Eggs with Braised Summer Vegetables

This is one of my favorite summertime meals! It varies with the pick of the day from the cooking school's garden.

ROASTING OVEN ENVIRONMENT

1 pound small zucchini
½ pound yellow crookneck squash (or any summer squash)
2 sweet green Italian peppers (may substitute with 1 red or yellow bell pepper)
2 shallots
1 clove garlic
6 fresh Roma tomatoes
¼ cup extra virgin olive oil
½ cup fresh basil leaves
1½ teaspoons kosher salt
8 eggs
¼ cup grated Parmigiano-Reggiano cheese
Pinch of red pepper flakes
Freshly ground black pepper

Rinse the zucchini and yellow squash, quarter lengthwise, and then cut into 1-inch pieces. Rinse peppers and dice to 1 inch; set aside. Peel the shallots and finely dice; mince the garlic.

Rinse the tomatoes, cut in half, and remove seeds. Coarsely chop and set aside with juices.

Set a casserole in the oven, add oil, and heat. Add shallots and cook for about 3 minutes, or until lightly browned and softened. Add garlic and cook for 1 minute. Do not burn. Add basil, stirring to heat, coat, and infuse oil. Add squash and peppers and cook for about 6–8 minutes. Vegetables should be lightly browned but still firm. Add tomatoes with their juices and salt. Cook uncovered for about 10–15 minutes. Sauce should be slightly thickened and the vegetables softened.

Pull casserole forward in the oven. Use a ladle to make an indentation in the vegetables for each egg. Crack eggs one at a time into a small bowl and slide into indentation. Cover casserole and return to oven for about 8–10 minutes, or until eggs have set. Sprinkle with Parmigiano-Reggiano, pepper flakes, and black pepper. Ladle eggs with plenty of vegetable sauce in individual bowls to serve.

SERVES 4

Frittata with Spring Onions, Asparagus, and Zucchini

Oven-baked frittatas served warm or cold can be enjoyed at brunch, lunch, or as an appetizer. This baked version is easy and allows you to use larger quantities for entertaining. Frittata is also another dish that can be changed seasonally with your favorite ingredients.

BAKE OVEN ENVIRONMENT

1 pound asparagus
1 pound zucchini
3 medium spring onions (may substitute
    with 1 medium sweet red onion)
2 tablespoons extra virgin olive oil
8 eggs
½ teaspoon salt
Freshly ground pepper
½ cup freshly grated Parmigiano-Reggiano
    cheese
1 teaspoon chopped fresh parsley
6 basil leaves, chiffonade

1 teaspoon grated lemon zest

Rinse the asparagus and remove the tough stem ends. Cut about 2 inches below the green tip and reserve asparagus tops. Cut remainder of stems into ¼-inch rounds.

Rinse the zucchini and cut in half lengthwise and then into ¼-inch slices.

Rinse the onions, cut in half lengthwise, and thinly slice.

Place a large sauté pan with the oil into the oven and heat. Add all the vegetables. Cook, stirring a few times, until lightly browned and softened. Remove and allow to cool.

Place the eggs, salt, pepper, Parmigiano-Reggiano, parsley, basil, and lemon zest in a mixing bowl and whisk lightly. Add the cooked vegetables to eggs and stir to combine. Pour egg mixture into an oiled 9 x 12-inch ceramic baking dish and set in the oven. Bake for about 15 minutes, or until puffed and golden on top, slightly firm when touched, and a knife inserted in the center comes out clean. Remove and allow to rest for 10 minutes. Cut into squares and serve.

SERVES 8

Frittata with Roasted Sweet Peppers, Fresh Oregano, and Provolone

BAKE OVEN ENVIRONMENT

2 red or yellow bell peppers, roasted
   (to roast, see page 68)
1 tablespoon extra virgin olive oil
1 clove garlic, minced
8 eggs
1 tablespoon chopped fresh oregano
1 teaspoon salt
Freshly grated black pepper
1 cup grated provolone cheese

Dice the peppers into $\frac{1}{2}$-inch pieces and toss with the oil and garlic. Set in a small sauté pan, place in oven, and heat through for about 1–2 minutes, stirring a few times, until garlic is fragrant. Do not burn. Remove and allow to cool.

Place the eggs, bell peppers, oregano, salt, and pepper in a bowl and whisk lightly. Stir in the provolone. Pour egg mixture into an oiled 9 x 12-inch ceramic baking dish and place in the oven. Bake for about 15 minutes, or until slightly firm when touched and a knife inserted in the center comes out clean. The top should be golden in color with bubbly melted cheese. Let rest for 10 minutes and then cut into squares and serve.

SERVES 8

Huevos Rancheros

3 strips applewood smoked bacon, cut into ½-inch pieces

1 red onion, small dice (about 2 cups)

1 red bell pepper, small dice (about 2 cups)

1 tablespoon finely diced jalapeño

3 (14-ounce) cans San Marzano tomatoes, with juices, crushed

1 (15-ounce) can black beans, rinsed and drained

1½ teaspoon salt

1 teaspoon ground cumin

1 teaspoon ground coriander

½ teaspoon smoked paprika

¼ teaspoon cayenne pepper

6–8 eggs

6 corn tortillas

1 cup grated smoked mozzarella cheese

3 tablespoons chopped cilantro

2 limes, cut into wedges

Place bacon in an 11-inch fry pan with a 2-½ inch side. Put into oven and cook until the fat renders and the bacon is beginning to brown, about 4 minutes.

Add the onion, bell pepper, and jalapeño and cook until very soft and starting to brown, about 12 minutes.

Add the tomatoes, beans, salt, and spices and stir to combine. Cook, uncovered, for 15 minutes more, or until heated through and bubbling.

With the back of a large spoon, make an indentation in the sauce and gently pour in a cracked egg. Repeat with the remaining eggs.

Cover tightly, return to oven and cook for about 8 minutes more, or until the whites are set.

Remove from the oven, leaving covered. Place the tortillas on a sheet pan in the oven and warm through, about 3 minutes.

To serve, put a tortilla on a plate, gently top with the sauce and an egg. Sprinkle on the cheese and cilantro and serve with a wedge of lime.

SERVES 6

BREAD

Basic Focaccia

Focaccia is a convenient and easy-to-make bread that satisfies with its salty olive oil flavor. Additionally, this basic recipe can be seasoned creatively with a variety of toppings. This recipe benefits from a lower bake temperature that can be done in either a bread or bake oven environment, which happens naturally every time you cook.

BREAD OVEN OR BAKE OVEN ENVIRONMENT

2½ teaspoons active dry yeast
1¾ cups warm water
5 cups all-purpose flour
2 teaspoons table salt
¾ cup extra virgin olive oil, divided
2 teaspoons coarse sea salt, for topping

In a small bowl, sprinkle the yeast over the warm water and let rest for 5 minutes to dissolve.

Place the flour and table salt in a large mixing bowl and stir to combine. Add yeast mixture and ½ cup oil and mix well until smooth but still soft and sticky, about 3 minutes.

Turn out onto a work surface and knead for about 5–8 minutes, adding a few tablespoons of flour if needed. The dough should remain soft but not sticky. Set dough in an oiled container, cover with plastic wrap, and set aside at room temperature to rise for 1½ hours. It should double in size.

Generously oil a half sheet pan and put dough on pan. Press and stretch dough with open hands to cover the bottom of the pan. Cover with a towel and allow to rest for 30 minutes. It should continue to rise and push out to fill the pan. Remove towel and, using the tips of your fingers, press across the entire surface of the dough to make dimples as deeply as you can without pressing through to the bottom of the pan. Cover dough with a towel and let rest for 30–45 minutes, or until it doubles in height.

Drizzle the remaining oil over the dough and sprinkle with the sea salt; set in oven to bake. Watch carefully to prevent the dough from over browning on the top. Cover loosely with foil if necessary. Bake for 30–40 minutes.

SERVES 12

Focaccia with Fresh Sage

BAKE OVEN ENVIRONMENT

Basic Focaccia (page 164)
1 cup fresh sage leaves

Rinse and dry sage leaves and coarsely chop.

Prepare the Basic Focaccia. Incorporate sage into the dough during the second 5–8 minute kneading process. Follow remainder of instructions in the basic recipe and bake as directed.

SERVES 12

Focaccia with Olives

BAKE OVEN ENVIRONMENT

Basic Focaccia (page 164)
1½ cups pitted olives, coarsely chopped
½ cup pitted olives, left whole

Prepare the Basic Focaccia.

Sprinkle pitted olives over dough during the second 5–8 minute kneading process and mix thoroughly into dough. Follow remainder of instructions in the basic recipe. Just before topping the dough with oil and sea salt, press the whole olives into the top of the focaccia. Bake as directed.

SERVES 12

Focaccia with Onions and Thyme

BAKE OVEN ENVIRONMENT

2 medium sweet onions, cut in half and
    sliced paper thin
2 tablespoons extra virgin olive oil
1 teaspoon finely chopped fresh thyme
2 teaspoons coarse sea salt
Basic Focaccia (page 164)

Place onions in a bowl and drizzle with the oil,
thyme, and sea salt; toss to coat.

Prepare the Basic Focaccia. Top with the onion
mixture, drizzle with the ¼ cup oil called for in
the basic recipe and omit the sea salt from the
basic recipe as well, as the 2 teaspoons of sea
salt are in the onion mixture. Bake as directed.

SERVES 12

Pane Toscano

Travelers to our cooking class in Tuscany often remark how bland the basic Tuscan bread Pane Toscano can taste. However, with its characteristic "little or no salt," it allows for maximum flexibility to season when incorporating it into other recipes such as crostini and ribollita. Additionally, its dense texture is perfect for grilling bruschetta, as it holds all that delicious olive oil!

BREAD OVEN ENVIRONMENT

BIGA
1 cup warm water
¼ teaspoon active dry yeast
1½ cups bread flour

DOUGH
1½ cups warm water, divided
1 teaspoon active dry yeast
3½ cups bread flour
½ teaspoon salt

Biga

Pour the water into a small mixing bowl, sprinkle with the yeast, and set aside for a few minutes to dissolve. Add flour and stir well to combine. Cover with plastic wrap and set out at room temperature overnight.

Dough

Pour the water in a large mixing bowl and sprinkle with yeast. Let rest for a few minutes until the yeast has dissolved. Add the Biga to the yeast mixture and mix well to combine.

Combine the flour and salt together and start adding to the yeast mixture, about ½ cup at a time, stirring continuously for about 5 minutes.

Turn out onto a floured work surface and knead for 10–12 minutes, or until smooth and elastic.

Set dough in an oiled container covered with plastic wrap and leave out at room temperature for about 1½ hours, or until doubled in size. Turn the dough out onto a floured work surface and divide in half. Place each half into a floured oval bread banneton (about 10 x 6 inches) to shape and rise. Cover with a towel and set aside for about 1½ hours. When ready to bake, turn banneton over onto a floured wood peel and slide the loaf onto the oven floor. Bake for about 25–30 minutes at 450°F.

YIELD 2 LOAVES

DESSERTS

Most of these recipes

include fresh fruit. Over the years we have experienced that the high moist heat in the oven accentuates the caramelization of the sugars in the fruit, making the wood-burning oven ideal for desserts.

Select your recipe based on seasonal availability and enjoy these delicious oven-baked desserts as the final course in your meal. Just let the flames die down after the higher heat that is required for your first and second courses, and you will be ready to bake a dessert that needs no additional firing.

Caramelized Pears with Crème Fraîche

BAKE OVEN ENVIRONMENT

2 tablespoons unsalted butter

3 tablespoons sugar

3 pears, peeled and quartered lengthwise (firm varieties of pears such as Comice or Anjou work better than the softer Bartlett)

½ teaspoon orange zest

¼ cup Cointreau, or any other orange-flavored liqueur

3 mint leaves, chiffonade

½ cup crème fraîche

In a sauté pan large enough to hold the pears in a single layer, melt the butter and sugar together, stirring occasionally to caramelize. Add the pears and cook for 6 minutes, turning gently as they brown. Add the zest, Cointreau, and mint and continue to cook for 3–4 minutes more, or until heated through. Pears should be tender when pierced and the caramel mixture golden. To serve, drizzle with crème fraîche.

SERVES 6

Roasted Figs with Fromage Blanc and Grated Chocolate

This is the simplest of recipes and is best with ripe figs oozing their natural sugars. The fast bake time can be done at almost any oven temperature.

BAKE OVEN OR ROASTING OVEN ENVIRONMENT

2 dozen fresh ripe figs

¼ cup fromage blanc

1 ounce semisweet chocolate

Stem the figs and then score the tops with a ¼-inch-deep "X." Set the figs in a ceramic baking dish and roast for about 3–4 minutes, or until they begin to release their juices and caramelize. Remove from the oven and place on a platter. Top each fig with ½ teaspoon fromage blanc and grate the chocolate over top.

YIELDS 24

Fresh Peach Crisp

🐟 BAKE OVEN ENVIRONMENT

TOPPING

2 cups whole raw almonds
1 stick unsalted butter, cut into 1-inch squares
½ cup packed brown sugar
¼ cup all-purpose flour

PEACHES

3 pounds ripe peaches, skin on and cut into
   1-inch pieces
¼ cup sugar
½ teaspoon cinnamon

Place the almonds in the bowl of a food processor and process until roughly chopped. Add the butter, sugar, and flour and continue to process until a crumbly mixture forms; set aside.

In a large bowl, toss the peaches with the sugar and cinnamon. Place peaches in a ceramic baking dish and sprinkle 2 cups topping over top.

Temper the ceramic dish by placing it in the mouth of the oven and turning to heat all sides for about 3 minutes. When the dish is hot, slide into the oven and cook until the peaches are heated through and the topping is beginning to brown, about 20 minutes. If the topping starts to brown quickly, cover loosely with foil.

Variation: Apple Crisp

Replace the peaches with 3 pounds Granny Smith apples, peeled and thinly sliced. Increase sugar to ½ cup and add ⅛ teaspoon grated nutmeg along with the ½ teaspoon cinnamon. Proceed as directed and bake for 30 minutes.

SERVES 8

Limoncello Bread Pudding with Fresh Blackberries

This fun recipe combines the famous Italian liqueur Limoncello with an all-American bread pudding.

BAKE OVEN ENVIRONMENT

1 (16-ounce) loaf brioche, crust removed and
    cut into 1-inch cubes
1 tablespoon butter
3 cups half-and-half
1¼ cups sugar, divided
1 tablespoon lemon zest
¼ teaspoon salt
6 large eggs
1 teaspoon vanilla extract
½ cup Limoncello
2 tablespoons lemon juice
10 ounces frozen blackberries, or fresh if
    in season (about 2 cups)
2 teaspoons cornstarch
Limoncello Topping (see below)

LIMONCELLO TOPPING
½ cup heavy cream
½ cup crème fraîche
1 tablespoon Limoncello
1 tablespoon plus 1 teaspoon sugar
1 teaspoon lemon juice

Divide the bread between two sheet pans. Toast in the oven until dry and lightly browned. Set aside to cool and then put in a large bowl.

Butter a 10 x 10-inch ceramic baking pan. Place the half-and-half, 1 cup sugar, lemon zest, and salt in a medium saucepan and heat just until the sugar is dissolved.

Crack the eggs into a large bowl. Slowly whisk the warm half-and-half mixture into eggs. Whisk until fully incorporated and then add the vanilla, Limoncello, and lemon juice; stir to combine.

Pour the custard mixture over the bread cubes and gently press bread to submerge in custard; let soak for 30–60 minutes.

Place the berries in a medium bowl. Toss with the remaining sugar and cornstarch and pour into mixing bowl with the bread cubes. Gently stir the berries into the mixture, being careful not to break up the bread. Pour entire contents of mixing bowl into buttered baking dish.

Place in the oven and bake for 25–30 minutes, or until browned, puffed, and set in the middle. Serve warm with Limoncello Topping.

Limoncello Topping

Place all of the ingredients in a medium bowl and whip until stiff peaks form. Refrigerate if not using right away.

SERVES 8

Cherry Clafouti

Serving this classic dessert warm from your wood-burning oven makes it even more enjoyable.

BAKE OVEN ENVIRONMENT

1 tablespoon butter

1 cup milk

1/4 cup cream

2/3 cup sugar, divided

4 eggs

2 tablespoons cherry liqueur

1/2 teaspoon vanilla extract

1/8 teaspoon salt

2/3 cup all-purpose flour

1 pound frozen pitted cherries, or
    fresh if in season

2 teaspoons cornstarch

Powdered sugar, for dusting

Whipped Topping, optional (see below)

WHIPPED TOPPING

8 ounces cream cheese, softened

1/2 cup sugar

2 tablespoons cherry liqueur

1/2 teaspoon vanilla extract

2 cups heavy cream

Butter a 10 x 10-inch ceramic baking dish.

Put the milk, cream, 1/3 cup sugar, eggs, liqueur, vanilla, salt, and flour in a blender. Blend for 30 seconds to combine.

Toss the cherries, remaining sugar, and cornstarch in a small bowl and transfer to the prepared baking dish. Spread the fruit evenly over the bottom of the dish and then gently pour the custard mixture over top. Place in oven and bake for 30–35 minutes, or until just puffed, browned, and set in the middle. The clafouti will deflate as it cools, so, if possible, serve warm directly from the oven, dusted with powdered sugar or a dollop of the topping.

Whipped Topping

Combine the cream cheese, sugar, liqueur, and extract in the bowl of a stand mixer. At medium speed, beat the mixture until softened and well combined. While the mixer is running, gradually add the heavy cream and whip until stiff peaks form.

SERVES 8

Rustic Crostada with Apples

The use of dried fruit in this recipe is especially nice during the fall, when fewer fresh fruits are available at the market. Make sure to prepare the pastry dough ahead of time!

BAKE OVEN ENVIRONMENT

4 Granny Smith apples, sliced ⅛ inch
½ cup chopped dates
¾ cup chopped dried apricots
3 tablespoons chopped crystallized ginger
1 tablespoon orange zest
2 tablespoons orange juice
½ cup plus 1 tablespoon sugar, divided
½ teaspoon cinnamon
¼ cup all-purpose flour
Pâte Brisée (see below)
2 tablespoons heavy cream
1 tablespoon unsalted butter
Powdered sugar, for dusting

PÂTE BRISÉE (PASTRY DOUGH)

1¾ cups unbleached all-purpose flour
1 teaspoon salt
1¼ sticks (5 ounces) chilled butter, cut into
    ¼-inch pieces
2 tablespoons (1 ounce) chilled shortening
    (cut into small pieces)
¼ to ½ cup ice water

In a large bowl, combine the apples, dried fruits, ginger, zest, juice, ½ cup sugar, and cinnamon. Toss to coat; set aside.

Wet your work surface with a few tablespoons of water. Place a piece of parchment paper on the damp counter; press down to smooth and adhere. Sprinkle parchment with a little flour and place the Pâte Brisée on top. Place rolling pin in the middle and roll away from you to the farthest pastry edge. Turn the pastry a quarter turn and repeat motion. Continue rolling until you have a 14-inch circle, adding more flour when necessary to keep the pastry from sticking.

Place the fruit in the middle of the dough, leaving 3–4 inches around the edge. Fold the dough up over the filling, pleating as you go. There will be a 4–5-inch circle of exposed filling when you are finished. Brush the pastry with the cream and sprinkle with remaining sugar. Dot the exposed filling with pieces of butter.

Trim the parchment to within 4 inches of the pastry. Slide wooden pizza peel under the parchment and transfer to the oven. Close the oven door. Bake for 15 minutes. Open the oven door and use the metal peel to lift the crostada up off of the parchment and then set it directly onto the floor of the oven. Discard the parchment paper. Close the oven door and cook for about 15–20 minutes more, or until the apples are soft and the pastry is browned and cooked through. Remove the crostada to a rack and let cool slightly. Dust with powdered sugar.

Pâte Brisée (Pastry Dough)

Place the flour and salt in the bowl of a food processor; pulse to mix. Add the butter and shortening and pulse until mixture resembles coarse cornmeal. Pour in ice water a few teaspoons at a time and pulse for a few seconds, until dough roughly comes together. Remove the dough, place on a work surface, and gather into a ball. Press into a thick disc about 4–5 inches in diameter. Flour lightly, wrap with plastic, and refrigerate for at least 2 hours or overnight.

SERVES 12

Fig, Walnut, and Chocolate Torte

This cake is delicious, even one or two days after being baked. It is not too sweet and is great enjoyed as a snack with a cup of coffee.

8 tablespoons unsalted butter, melted and cooled, divided

3/4 cup plus 1 tablespoon all-purpose flour

1 cup coarsely chopped dried figs

1 1/2 cups chopped walnuts

4 large eggs

1/3 cup plus 2 tablespoons sugar

1 teaspoon vanilla extract

1 1/2 teaspoons baking powder

1/3 cup chopped bittersweet chocolate

1 teaspoon fennel seeds

Powdered sugar, for dusting

Brush the inside of a 9-inch cake pan with 1/2 tablespoon melted butter. Line the bottom of the pan with a piece of parchment paper and brush the paper with another 1/2 tablespoon butter. Add 1 tablespoon flour and shake pan to coat completely.

Combine the figs and walnuts in a bowl and sprinkle over the bottom of the prepared pan, covering evenly.

Beat the eggs and sugar in a large bowl until creamy; add the remaining butter and vanilla.

Sift the remaining flour and baking powder into a small bowl. Fold in the chocolate. Using a wooden spoon, add the flour mixture to the egg mixture and stir to combine. Stir in the fennel seeds and pour batter evenly over the figs and walnuts. Place in the oven for 20 minutes. Check after 10 minutes—if the nuts are getting too brown, lay a piece of oiled foil over the top. The torte is done when a toothpick inserted into the center comes out clean. Cool for 20 minutes on a wire rack. Place the rack over the pan upside down and invert. Remove the cake pan and peel off the parchment paper. Place a plate on the torte and quickly flip right side up. Once cooled, dust with powdered sugar and serve.

SERVES 8–10

Baked Apples with Fresh Caramel Sauce

BAKE OVEN ENVIRONMENT

4 large baking apples (Granny Smith,
   Rome, Jonagold, Pippin, Gala, Braeburn,
   or Gravenstein)
1/3 cup brown sugar
1 teaspoon cinnamon
1/4 cup chopped nuts
1/3 cup diced dried fruit, such as raisins,
   apricots, or cranberries
1 tablespoon butter, divided in fourths
1 cup apple juice
Caramel Sauce (see below)

CARAMEL SAUCE

1 cup sugar
1/4 cup water
3/4 cup heavy cream
6 tablespoons unsalted butter, room temperature
1 tablespoon dark rum, optional

With a paring knife, remove stems and cores of the apples to 1/2 inch of the bottom. Carve the openings about 1 inch round.

Combine the sugar, cinnamon, nuts, and dried fruit in a small bowl.

Place the apples in a small ceramic baking pan and fill the hollowed centers with the sugar and fruit mixture; top with butter. Add the apple juice to the bottom of the pan. Cover tightly with a lid or foil and bake for about 30 minutes. Test an apple for doneness by piercing with the tip of a knife. Do not overcook or the apples will be mushy. Baste apples with the pan juices. Serve with vanilla ice cream and drizzle with the Caramel Sauce.

Caramel Sauce

Place the sugar and water in a heavy-bottom saucepan. Do not stir. Place in the oven for about 20–25 minutes, checking occasionally and gently swirling the pan to incorporate the melting sugar. When the sugar has turned a dark golden brown, slowly add the cream—it will bubble vigorously. Stir with a wooden spoon to mix the cream into the sugar. The sugar will harden. Place back into the oven for about 1–2 minutes to re-melt the caramel. Remove from the oven and add the butter, stirring to incorporate, and then add the rum, if using. If there are hardened bits of sugar, pass through a strainer to remove.

SERVES 4

Tuscan-Style Rustic Apple Cake

In our cooking school, the students felt the leftover cake served cold from the refrigerator the following day was equally as good!

BAKE OVEN ENVIRONMENT

1 stick unsalted butter, melted and cooled, divided

$\frac{1}{2}$ cup plus 1 tablespoon unbleached all-purpose flour, divided

5 Golden Delicious apples

2 large eggs

1$\frac{1}{4}$ cups sugar

$\frac{1}{2}$ cup whole milk

1 teaspoon vanilla extract

2 teaspoons baking powder

Powdered sugar, for dusting

Use $\frac{1}{2}$ tablespoon melted butter to brush the inside of a 9-inch cake pan. Line the bottom of the pan with a piece of parchment paper and brush the paper with another $\frac{1}{2}$ tablespoon butter. Add 1 tablespoon flour and shake pan to coat completely.

Peel, core, and quarter the apples. Slice the sections crosswise into very thin slices; set aside.

Beat the eggs and sugar in a large bowl with a whisk until the sugar is dissolved and the eggs are pale yellow. Stir in the remaining flour and then add the milk, remaining butter, and vanilla. Blend the mixture, but do not overwork. Stir in the baking powder and fold in the apples.

Pour the mixture into the prepared pan and bake for 40–45 minutes. Check after 20 minutes and loosely cover with oiled foil if it is browning too quickly. The cake is done when a small paring knife inserted in the center comes out clean.

Cool the cake on a wire rack for 20 minutes. Place the rack over the pan upside down and invert. Remove the cake pan and peel off the parchment paper. Cool 15 minutes more and then place a plate on the cake and quickly flip the cake right side up. Dust with powdered sugar and serve.

SERVES 8–10

Biscotti di Prato

Enjoy classic biscotti warm from the oven with a glass of your favorite Vin Santo.

LOWEST BAKING ENVIRONMENT

4 whole large eggs, plus 1 egg white

1½ cups sugar

1 teaspoon vanilla extract

¼ cup extra virgin olive oil

Pinch of salt

2 tablespoons anise seed

2 cups raw whole almonds

4 cups cake flour, plus more for kneading

1½ teaspoons baking powder

Place the whole eggs, sugar, vanilla, oil, salt, and anise into a bowl and mix well. Fold in the almonds. Combine 4 cups flour and the baking powder in a second bowl and mix well. Add the flour mixture to the egg mixture a little at a time, mixing after each addition to incorporate. Once the dough comes together and isn't too sticky, turn out onto a lightly floured work surface and knead gently, adding a little more flour if necessary. Divide into three portions and roll each piece into a log about 3 x 10 inches long, and set on an oiled sheet pan.

Beat the egg white with a fork until frothy; brush onto logs. Bake at 350°F in the oven for 30–40 minutes. Remove from oven and let cool slightly before cutting into 1-inch-thick diagonal slices.

MAKES APPROXIMATELY 30 BISCOTTI

Index

Metric Conversion Chart

Volume Measurements		Weight Measurements		Temperature Conversion	
U.S.	METRIC	U.S.	METRIC	FAHRENHEIT	CELSIUS
1 teaspoon	5 ml	½ ounce	15 g	250	120
1 tablespoon	15 ml	1 ounce	30 g	300	150
¼ cup	60 ml	3 ounces	90 g	325	160
⅓ cup	75 ml	4 ounces	115 g	350	180
½ cup	125 ml	8 ounces	225 g	375	190
⅔ cup	150 ml	12 ounces	350 g	400	200
¾ cup	175 ml	1 pound	450 g	425	220
1 cup	250 ml	2¼ pounds	1 kg	450	230